D1061986

COMPTOIR LIBANAIS

FEASTS FROM THE MIDDLE EAST

TONY KITOUS

COMPTOIR LIBANAIS

# FEASTS FROM THE MIDDLE EAST

TONY KITOUS

HQ

HQ
An imprint of HarperCollinsPublishers Ltd
1 London Bridge Street
London SE1 9GF

10 9 8 7 6 5 4 3 2 1

First published in Great Britain by HQ
An imprint of HarperCollinsPublishers Ltd
2018

Copyright © Tony Kitous 2018

Tony Kitous asserts the moral right to
be identified as the author of this work.
A catalogue record for this book is
available from the British Library.

ISBN 978-0-00-824834-5

Our policy is to use papers that are natural,
renewable and recyclable products and
made from wood grown in sustainable
forests. The logging and manufacturing
processes conform to the legal environmental
regulations of the country of origin.
For more information visit:
www.harpercollins.co.uk/green

Photography: Philippa Langley
Food styling: Rosie Ramsden
Prop styling: Olivia Wardle
Design & Art Direction: Anita Mangan
Senior Commissioning Editor: Rachel Kenny
Project Editor: Sarah Hammond
Head of Design: Louise McGrory

Printed and bound in China by
RR Donnelley

All rights reserved. No part of this
publication may be reproduced, stored
in a retrieval system, or transmitted, in
any form or by any means, electronic,
mechanical, photocopying, recording or
otherwise, without the prior permission of
the publishers.

This book is sold subject to the condition
that it shall not, by way of trade or otherwise,
be lent, re-sold, hired out or otherwise
circulated without the publisher's prior
consent in any form of binding or cover
other than that in which it is published and
without a similar condition including this
condition being imposed on the subsequent
purchaser.

# CONTENTS

INTRODUCTION                          6
MIDDLE EASTERN STORE CUPBOARD        11

BREAKFAST & BREADS                   16
MEZZE & DIPS                         52
SALADS & VEGETABLES                  88
ROASTS & GRILLS                      120
FISH & SEAFOOD                       138
SOUPS & STEWS                        154
GRAINS & PULSES                      180
DESSERTS & DRINKS                    206

FEAST MENUS                          246
INDEX                                250
ACKNOWLEDGEMENTS                     256

I like food – in fact, I love food. I love absolutely everything about food: the smells, the tastes, the colours, the way it makes people happy. A simple smell can take me back to the markets I used to go to with my dad and grandad to buy ingredients for my mum. Or it can transport me back to walking home from school, smelling the food in the air when I was close to home. I remember men walking the streets with their carts of sardines shouting, 'Yalla sardine!' and everybody going out to buy them. Every family cooked and flavoured them differently. We'd eat at home and then take the leftovers outside to swap with our friends. I can recall the aroma of fruit ripening on the trees, too. To this day, no matter where I am, a new-season fig will make me close my eyes to savour that first bite, longing to be six years old again, back in Tizi Ouzou, Algeria.

Since I was little it has always been the same. I ate so much so that my mum used to hide food because otherwise it would be gone! Always, always eating. I learned about the joys of food from my mum, Zohra. She is my inspiration, my motivation in everything I do and my biggest influence. She taught me the joy of eating, of feeding people and of learning about new foods. My mother was the heart of the home, cooking for hours every day. She was very creative when meat or fish were scarce or there were lots of people to feed (I'm the oldest of seven). I also came to realise that no matter how simple, food can always be delicious when it's made with love and with fresh, seasonal ingredients.

As food was such a big part of everyday life when I was growing up, it wasn't long before I started to think, dream and talk about food. I was brought up in both a Berber

and Arab culture and have embraced both my whole life. The Middle East and North Africa are lands of generous hospitality, and people often don't see the inclusive nature of Arab culture, with eating at the heart of it. Food is an integral part of my roots; food is everything because you give it and share it and you make it with love. Eating it offers a chance to be with friends and family, to talk and laugh and celebrate and share the latest news. Food brings us together.

As a child I was spoilt by my grandma, who would cook all the things I liked. My grandparents kept chickens, and sometimes I'd go there in my lunch break and run down the garden to see if there were any eggs. I would collect the eggs and take them to the kitchen where grandma would cook them simply by frying them in some extra-virgin olive oil, with a little garlic and some coriander – there might be some aubergines or potatoes, too. I'd pick plums, pomegranates and figs straight from the tree, plump and juicy and ripened by the hot sun.

I started earning my own money at a young age. We lived across the street from the big football ground. I would get up early to buy tickets for a match and sell them later to visitors from out of town – at a slightly inflated price! My mum would help me make lemonade or merguez sandwiches, which I'd sell on the street. My father never knew as he wouldn't have approved of his son selling things on the street. This was my street life and a big part of my education. Working on the streets of Tizi Ouzou taught me that you could make opportunities for yourself.

By the time I was nine I was hitch-hiking up to the coast, about half an hour away, during

the summer holidays, where I helped the fishermen with their catches – emptying the nets, cleaning the fish – not for money, but because I liked to do it. My parents thought I was staying with friends, but really I was exploring and looking for the next adventure.

As I grew older, my desire to see and experience more took me further afield. At 15 I used my savings to visit Tunisia, at 16 I ventured to Spain and at 17, it was France. Every year I worked a little harder, saved a little more and travelled a little further. I had just turned 18 when my friend Nasser and I decided that we would travel to London. I arrived with £70 in my pocket (£50 of which was borrowed from my uncle). We spent our first night in Victoria Station, unsure where to go and needing to make our little money last. I fell in love with the city over that summer and ended up living in a squat in Manor House, working wherever I could.

I returned home the day before I was due to start university. I made it through half an hour of my first engineering lecture before I walked out, knowing it wasn't for me. I'd had a taste of something else and I wanted more. My parents didn't want me to go – it was unusual for the first-born son to leave the family like this. They roped in uncles, cousins and family friends to talk me out of it, although this just made me more determined to go. But I couldn't leave without a letter from my father stamped by the police, as I was only 18. And, most importantly, I wanted to go with their blessings.

In the end, he gave me that letter, despite the reservations he must still have had about his eldest son leaving to live in London, with no job or home and only basic English. This was

an incredibly difficult decision for him and I thank him for it every day, even though he is no longer with us.

I left as soon as I could. But I hadn't expected the huge weight of responsibility that I felt the minute I passed through the doors of Heathrow. I realised that I had to make this choice count. I had to make my family proud and make something of myself if I wasn't going to university. Within four years I needed to have a restaurant. I had to start working hard – and quickly!

For the next few years I worked two full-time jobs every day in pubs, bars and restaurants from 6 a.m. until late. I returned to the squat to live initially but then I was offered a live-in job at a small hotel. Hot running water, my own bed and breakfast every day! I stayed focused on my goal of having my own restaurant for the next four years.

I was working in a restaurant on Wigmore Street when one day I turned up to find it closed. The rent hadn't been paid and the landlord had taken back the property. This was my chance. I had enough money in the bank for a deposit and a few months' rent. I set up a meeting and bought myself a suit and tie, ready to impress.

It went well, and it was agreed that I could take on the restaurant, but one clause in the lease worried my lawyer and so he advised against it. I called a friend of my uncle, who had lived in England for some time, to ask his advice. After listening to all that I had to say he asked how old I was and what I had to lose. When I answered 'Twenty-two', and 'Nothing', he said, 'Then you have your answer.'

I signed that contract and today, some 25 years later, I still have that restaurant on Wigmore Street.

I want you to fall in love with the Middle East and its bold flavours and welcoming, generous traditions. Maybe it will once again become the place to travel to, but in the meantime, these flavours are becoming an integral part of the food landscape. I want to share them with you. The food of the Middle East is the best in the world.

As Middle Eastern food grows in popularity, ingredients that were once hard to source are now readily available. I've always wanted everyone to be able to cook these amazing recipes at home, which is why I set up the souk shops within our restaurants, so you can buy orange blossom water or za'atar.

The recipes in this book allow you to put together your own feasts, whether you are two, ten or twenty people; whether you want breakfast, brunch, lunch, dinner or anything in between. For example, I love a selection of dishes for breakfast, but if I'm in a hurry I make the Aubergine & Halloumi Omelette (page 20), a delicious start to any day.

Mezze is how we welcome guests into our homes – the more the better! I can't choose a favourite as I love everything about the way mezze encourages everyone to join in and share. You will never walk away from an Arabic table hungry! In addition, there is always a salad of some kind, and as a lover of aubergines, Grilled Chopped Aubergine Salad (page 90) has a huge place in my heart.

One of my favourite recipes is the Slow-cooked Shoulder of Lamb (page 124), cooked with herbs and spices, rice and dried fruits.

It's something you can build a feast around. And My Mum Zohra's Fried Sardines (page 146) is still my favourite fish dish and never fails to make me feel nostalgic.

Soups and stews are a huge part of the Middle Eastern diet. My mum made sure there was soup on the table every day in winter; my favourite today is Artichoke & Tahina Soup (page 159). Soups can be eaten on their own or enjoyed alongside recipes such as Giant Couscous with Chicken (page 204) and some roast vegetables.

No feast is complete without something sweet to finish! I like to play with flavours and experiment with ways of using ingredients. My Roasted Aubergine, Rose Honey & Labneh Tart (page 234) is one of those special recipes that is truly unique. Dipping pastries into café crème, or refreshing yourself with a lemonade or mint tea, is also part of Arabic culture, as the days can be very hot and the evenings cool.

I feel fortunate to be able to do this wonderful job for a living. It is a job I love, and it doesn't feel like work when you love what you do and when you are making a home from home – an extended family. These recipes and restaurants are more than a reflection of me; they are manifestations of my experiences - from the flavours on the menus to the designs on the walls. Comptoir Libanais is everything to me: my memories, my life, my culture, my family, my children. The people who dine with us aren't customers, but guests in our home – and you are all very welcome.

Sahtein! (simply, 'Enjoy your food!')

Tony

# MIDDLE EASTERN STORE CUPBOARD

Middle Eastern ingredients are very versatile and can be used in lots of different ways. They're easier to find now, but when I first came to London in the late 1980s they used to be much harder to source – I found it difficult even to buy couscous! Since opening Comptoir Libanais, I've stocked all sorts of products, such as jams, oils and orange blossom water, just as you would find in a souk, so our guests can buy them easily. Here are the ingredients I always have in, with which you can easily rustle up a delicious meal.

## ALLSPICE

If I want a little bit more warmth in my food, I'll add a pinch or two of allspice. You can also buy these little brown peppercorns ground, which I find easier to use. The seeds are picked, unripe, from the pimento tree and have a unique flavour - a mixture of cinnamon, cloves, nutmeg and pepper. Try it in Spiced Lamb Koftas with Potatoes & Tomatoes (page 166).

## BLACK PEPPERCORNS

Sometimes I wonder what I'd do without salt and pepper. Food that is not seasoned at all (or not seasoned enough) tastes bland, as the seasoning helps to enhance the flavour of all the ingredients and bring them together. In the restaurants we always throw a good pinch or two of black pepper into a pan of bones bubbling in liquid when making stocks. And, of course, peppercorns can be crushed into pieces, as big or as small as you like, for seasoning.

## BULGAR WHEAT

We also call this burghul or cracked wheat, and you can buy it finely ground, medium or coarse. The fine version is brilliant in salads (see my very easy Bulgar Wheat & Tomato Salad, page 198), but you can also use the other varieties to give texture to a dish such as Potato & Spiced Minced Lamb Pie (page 178).

## CARAWAY

I use ground caraway in the flavoursome chicken recipe, Giant Couscous with Chicken (page 204). This powerful, musky-tasting spice is as divisive as Marmite – some people love it, some hate it. You can also buy the seeds (they're a similar shape to cumin seeds), which are often used to garnish bread.

## CARDAMOM

I love the delicate scent that cardamom brings to a dish. The spice is encased in a shell and it's the black seeds hiding within that you need. Crush the pods by carefully placing a large chopping knife on top of them and pushing down on the knife with your fist until you hear a little crack. Take the seeds out and use them as described in the recipe. Cardamom adds a delicate flavour to Café Blanc (page 237).

## CHICKPEAS

These are a must, must, must in my cupboard! Dried chickpeas are best for making Hommos (page 56), as they produce a much better flavour and texture than tinned ones, as well as in falafel (check out my Feta & Nigella Seed Falafel recipe, page 82). Like dried lentils, chickpeas are much cheaper dried than tinned. You just need to remember to soak them first – about 4–6 hours is enough, or overnight. I buy tinned ful (fava beans) though (see opposite).

## CHILLI FLAKES & CHILLI POWDER

I love chillies – they're up there with sumac and za'atar as one of my favourite spices. Both the flakes and the powder pack a punch, so I use them sparingly. Middle Eastern food is not about high levels of spice, more a subtle balance of flavours that all work together. I use both chilli flakes and fresh chillies in Aleppo Roast Peppers & Mixed Nut Dip (page 70) to add two slightly different flavours to the recipe. Chilli powder works better when blended with other ingredients, such as when seasoning the flour for the Spiced Fried Squid recipe (page 74).

## CIDER VINEGAR

If you have good olive oil and cider vinegar in your store cupboard, you'll always be able to make a great dressing. I sometimes mix it with lemon juice, so there's a little sweetness to the taste, too.

## CINNAMON

This spice is often used in both sweet and savoury recipes. I pop cinnamon sticks into Giant Couscous with Chicken (page 204) and sweet recipes (see Labneh with Caramelised Poached Quinces & Spiced Dried Fruit, page 40), in which the stick can withstand long periods of simmering. Use ground cinnamon when blending this spice with other ingredients, for example in the Sweet Potato & Tahina Pudding (page 216).

## CORIANDER

We don't use the spice coriander in our cooking nearly as much as we do the fresh herb or even cumin, but it still serves a purpose. The slightly lemony flavour of the spice will soften and complement other ingredients, such as the cumin in the Feta & Nigella Seed Falafel (page 82).

## COUSCOUS

When I was young, I remember my mum buying couscous in very large bags – they'd be either 25kg or 50kg – as we used to eat so much of it. Gone are the days when it was always steamed in a couscoussier (the traditional steamer used in the Middle East to cook couscous). This method does make the texture really light, but it's quicker to pour hot water or stock over the grains and leave them to soak for 10–15 minutes to rehydrate them. Couscous needs lots of flavouring – oil and lemon juice, and you can also melt a knob of butter in the hot liquid – and then it's ready to serve with rich stews. A lighter recipe, and very delicious, is my favourite Roasted Chicken & Couscous Salad (page 86).

## CUMIN

This spice infuses any recipe with a distinctive musky flavour. It's often used with coriander, which complements it perfectly, with its lemony character. It's a must in My Mum Zohra's Fried Sardines (page 146). Buy cumin seeds if you have a good spice grinder, or use ground cumin if you need to save time.

## FREEKEH

We don't use this as often as couscous or bulgar wheat, but I do enjoy it and it's delicious in my easy and very filling Freekeh with Chicken (page 196). Like bulgar and couscous, it is wheat, but it is harvested when young and green, then toasted and cracked to make the freekeh. It has a slightly nutty flavour and the cooking time varies depending on the packet you buy. Check this before you start so you don't end up with bullet-like grains when you're preparing it.

## DRIED FRUIT

I always keep dried dates, figs, prunes and apricots in my cupboard – they're instant snacks, plus I also love to serve them with mint tea and perhaps some whole almonds if anyone drops by. Much smaller dried fruit, such as sultanas, are also useful. Have a look at one of my favourite recipes, Slow-cooked Shoulder of Lamb (page 124), where I go to town with the whole range.

## FUL OR FAVA BEANS

I've explained why it's better to buy dried chickpeas and lentils, but I tend to buy ful or fava beans in tins. These are broad beans that have been dried then rehydrated. You can,

of course, cook the dried beans, but it takes more time, and the recipes I use them in – Ful Salad with Radish & Mint (page 112) and Broad Beans in a Tomato Sauce (page 34) – are quick to make, so it's easier to use tinned.

## HARISSA

I love this fiery hot paste and I've even been known to enjoy it on eggs for breakfast. It's also great swirled into yoghurt to make a dip, which softens its heat. You can buy it ready-made in jars or tubes (which makes it look a little like tomato purée), but I urge you to make my homemade harissa sauce, which is served with the Spiced Fried Squid (page 74) and keeps well in the fridge.

## HONEY

For me, sugar brings a simple sweetness to a recipe, but to give depth, too, you need a good-flavoured honey. We often use honey to make a syrup; I love using it this way, especially combined with orange blossom water or rose water. Choose a runny honey so it dissolves easily into other ingredients. it's wonderful in the Walnut & Cinnamon Honey Cigars (page 228).

## LEBANESE SEVEN-SPICE MIX

I use this to season a piece of meat when I want to add a little extra something, at the same time as salt and pepper. Seven-spice is a blend of allspice, black pepper, cinnamon, coriander, ginger, cloves and nutmeg. I use it in the Chicken & Chickpea Stew (page 176), and also to give a more powerful flavour to a finished dish, such as the Slow-cooked Shoulder of Lamb (page 124).

## DRIED LENTILS

These are really handy as they don't need soaking overnight, and a little goes a long way. I keep both green and red lentils in the cupboard. Lentils need extra herbs and spices to give them flavour and garlic is always a good addition. Try my budget-friendly Lentil Soup with Lemon (page 158), which uses a handful of ingredients and is bulked up with Swiss chard.

## DRIED MINT

We use dried herbs in dishes that need long, slow cooking as they have a more intense flavour than fresh herbs. The powerful flavour of dried mint can also be used to finish off a recipe, as in Stuffed Cabbage Leaves with Spiced Minced Lamb & Rice (page 200). The little parcels of cabbage stuffed with rice are drizzled with an aromatic herb and garlic butter.

## NIGELLA SEEDS

I like these little black seeds in the Feta & Nigella Seed Falafel (page 82) as they have a slightly bitter flavour, which enhances the herbs, spices and other ingredients. I also love the fact that they look good decorating the outside of the balls. If you're looking for them in supermarkets, you might see them labelled as black onion seeds or kalonji seeds.

## NUTS

Nuts play a big role in Middle Eastern food; they are part of our culture. If someone drops by, we put a bowl of nuts on the table. When we bake, we use them in sweet recipes. At the end of a meal, we'll finish with mint tea and a bowl of nuts and dried fruit. You can buy them everywhere – from stalls in the street to shops specialising in roasted seeds and nuts, so of course I like to use them generously in whatever dish I'm making. If you can, buy them in big bags – it's cheaper that way – and store them in a cool, dark cupboard so they don't go off. I like to keep a good range in stock, but pistachios and pine nuts are my favourites so I always have these in. Try pistachios in my Fig, Halloumi & Pistachio Tart (page 226) and sprinkle pine nuts over Feta & Spinach Flatbread (page 49).

## EXTRA-VIRGIN OLIVE OIL

I like my olive oil to have a rich colour and a deep flavour. Lots of people reserve extra-virgin olive oil for dressings, but if you can buy a reasonably priced one, it's worth cooking with it, too. The only time I use another oil is when I'm deep-frying, and then I use sunflower or vegetable oil, as they have high smoking points.

## PAPRIKA

This lovely, red, smooth-tasting spice is made by drying sweet red peppers then grinding them into a powder. It doesn't have any heat and is lovely in the mezze recipe, Aleppo Roast Peppers & Mixed Nut Dip (page 70).

## POMEGRANATE MOLASSES

I love this pink-hued syrup, which is a mixture of sweet and sour. It's quite powerful – a little goes a long way – so I tend to dot it carefully over salads. It's particularly good in the Spiced Lamb Pastries (page 78), in which the sweetness enhances the savoury filling of these little pies.

## RICE

Basmati is my go-to rice on the side if I'm serving a stew with lots of sauce, and it's essential in dishes in which light, fluffy rice is needed, for example, my Palestinian Spiced Rice with Chicken (page 184). Pudding rice isn't just used for desserts; we use this stubby variety in recipes where the rice part of a stuffing, as in the Stuffed Cabbage Leaves with Spiced Minced Lamb and Rice (page 200). The sticky nature of the grains helps to meld all the ingredients together and maintain the shape of the cabbage parcels.

## ROSE WATER AND ORANGE BLOSSOM WATER

I buy these scented waters in big bottles, as they are better value. I quite often advise the chefs not to be cautious about adding these waters to dishes. The orange blossom water adds a really interesting twist to the Date, Almond, Orange Blossom & Labneh Smoothie (page 242), while the rosewater is a must in the Roasted Aubergine, Rose, Honey & Labneh Tart (page 234).

## SALT

You'll notice that most of the recipes in this book specify a measured quantity of salt in the ingredients list. It's so important to season food properly as this helps to bring the flavours of all the ingredients together and enhance them. I like sea salt, but you may need to grind it to make it finer if you're making bread, so that it disperses through the flour properly.

## SESAME SEEDS

These tiny little seeds pack a punch once they're toasted – see my gorgeous breakfast feta recipes (pages 24–5). They also give a great texture to falafel or to finish off our renowned Sesame Seed Bread (page 50).

## SUMAC

This is one of my absolute favourite spices. I love the deep red colour and the lemony, slightly sour flavour. The bush that these berries come from originated in the Middle East. The berries are dried and ground into powder. A sprinkling is perfect with sweet-flavoured ingredients such as tomatoes, so try it in my Village Tomato Salad (page 100).

## TAHINA

Along with extra-virgin olive oil and pomegranate molasses, tahina is one of those store-cupboard ingredients that I have to keep in. I buy it in a big plastic tub – it's cheaper that way – and keep it in the cupboard next to the salt and pepper, so it's always to hand. You may spot it labelled as 'tahini' in supermarkets. Anyone close to me knows how much I love aubergines, so even simple dishes such as grilled or roasted aubergines are served with a drizzle of tahina over the top, to make them taste even better. I also love it in the amazing New Potatoes & Green Tahina Salad (page 98).

## ZA'ATAR

I couldn't live without za'atar, the spice blend of wild thyme, sesame seeds, sumac and salt, and I will add it to anything. It's a must on man'ousha (pages 48–9) and I particularly love it pressed into halloumi – see Za'atar-crusted Halloumi (page 84). Just so you know, we call wild dried thyme za'atar, too.

In the Middle East and North Africa we have a huge variety of breakfast dishes, from light tartine toasts to classic shakshuka. These are recipes to enjoy greedily on your own or share lazily with friends on the weekend.

# BREAKFAST & BREADS

My mum used to make this favourite of mine for me, my brothers and my sister. Breakfast was pretty busy for her with seven of us to feed, but she could rustle this up quickly and sometimes she made it for lunch instead. If she was really pressed for time, instead of waiting for the eggs to set, she'd scramble them into the tomato mixture, which I loved.

Here I've married the classic with one of my favourite ingredients, aubergine. You must make the sauce in an ovenproof frying pan, as the eggs are baked right at the end. Just 5 minutes in a hot oven is all it takes for the whites to set and the yolks to still be soft and runny.

# AUBERGINE SHAKSHUKA
## SHAKSHUKA BATENJAN

olive oil, for frying
2 large aubergines,
  sliced into rounds
½ red onion, sliced
1 garlic clove, finely
  chopped
8 large tomatoes on the
  vine, chopped
125ml tomato juice
½ tsp salt
½ tsp black pepper
½ tsp cumin (optional)
6 large eggs
100g feta cheese,
  roughly chopped

TO SERVE
a few parsley sprigs and
  a large mint sprig
warm pitta bread

Preheat the oven to 220°C/200°C fan/gas mark 7.

Heat 1 tablespoon of oil in a large frying pan. Season the aubergine slices and fry them in batches for 3–4 minutes on each side, until golden and tender, adding more oil as necessary. Transfer the slices to a plate as they are cooked.

Heat 2 tablespoons of oil in a medium frying pan and sauté the onion gently over a low-to-medium heat for about 8 minutes, stirring every now and then, until softened. Stir in the garlic and cook for a further minute.

Tip the tomatoes into the pan along with any juice and stir into the onion. Cook for 8 minutes until the tomatoes have broken down and softened – they should be a pulp. Pour in the tomato juice and cook, again over a low heat, for 5 minutes. The sauce will be quite thick by this stage. Season with salt, black pepper and the cumin, if using.

Spread a layer of aubergine slices over a large, ovenproof dish, then spoon over half the tomato sauce. Repeat to make two layers.

Make a hole in the sauce with the back of a large spoon and crack an egg into it. Do the same all round the dish until you've positioned all the eggs. Scatter over the feta. Bake in the oven for 5 minutes.

Pick the leaves off the parsley and mint sprigs, and chop roughly. Scatter over the shakshuka and serve with the warm pitta bread.

**SERVES 6**

This is a dish I had at a friend's house on the outskirts of Beirut. We were totally spoilt there as his mum would cook four or five different dishes for breakfast every morning, and because she knew I loved this, she would always make it. It's a big, open omelette, topped with tender chunks of aubergine, caramelised cherry tomatoes and bite-size cubes of halloumi – all seasoned with one of my favourite spice blends. If you want to get ahead with this to make it a really speedy dish to rustle up, you could cook the vegetables and cheese the day before and chill them. Just make sure you toss them in a pan to heat them through before topping the omelette.

# AUBERGINE & HALLOUMI OMELETTE
## BATENJAN WA HALLOUMI

3 tbsp olive oil, plus extra to drizzle
½ aubergine, chopped into 2cm cubes
za'atar, to season
100g cherry tomatoes, halved
75g halloumi, chopped
8 large eggs
salt and black pepper
fresh thyme, to serve

Heat the oven to 100°C/80°C fan/gas mark ¼ to keep the vegetables and halloumi warm while making the omelette.

Heat 2 tablespoons of oil in a large frying pan and cook the aubergine over a low heat, tossing every now and then until golden. Season with za'atar and some salt and pepper. Spoon into a roasting tin. Add the remaining tablespoon of oil to the pan and fry the tomatoes, cut-side down, until just golden and caramelised, but not squishy. Season in the same way as the aubergine and put in the tin.

Cook the halloumi in the pan, tossing it every now and then so that the cubes turn golden on each side and then season them, too. Spoon into the tin, then put the tin in the oven to keep warm.

Beat the eggs in a bowl and season well. Add a drizzle more oil to the pan and place over a low-to-medium heat. Pour in the beaten eggs.

As the egg starts to cook, draw a wooden spoon across the base of the pan to allow more of it to cook. It'll wrinkle up and make a much thicker – and more delicious – omelette this way. Lower the heat if it cooks too quickly and continue until the egg is just set on top. Spoon the aubergine, tomatoes and halloumi on top, garnish with fresh thyme and more za'atar, and serve.

SERVES 6

# FETA 4 WAYS
## JEBNA FETA

It's a bit unusual to have feta for breakfast, but I've been brought up on it and the salty, slightly sharp flavour goes brilliantly with both savoury and sweet ingredients. To be honest, I'm so greedy I could easily hoover up a block when it's served with any of the accompaniments here. Sometimes I use a handful of mixed nuts in place of pistachios, and toast them in a pan first for extra flavour. And, if I can get hold of them, I love it topped with candied figs and a drop of rose water. Fingers of hot, just-toasted pitta cut through the richness, and a bowl of fruit completes the meal. If you have any left over, save it for lunch and serve it in a sandwich. (See photos on pages 22-3.)

**EACH BLOCK OF FETA SERVES 4-6**

# FETA WITH TOMATOES & SPRING ONIONS

250g block of feta, cut
   into three equal pieces
3 tomatoes, halved,
   deseeded and chopped
3 spring onions, sliced
½-1 red chilli, sliced
small handful of flat-leaf
   parsley, chopped
black pepper, to season
olive oil, for drizzling
juice of ¼ large lemon
paprika, to sprinkle

Arrange the feta on a plate. Spoon over the tomatoes, spring onions, chilli and parsley. Season with black pepper – there's no need to add salt as the feta is salty.

Drizzle over some olive oil – about 2 tablespoons will be plenty – then squeeze over the lemon. Finally sprinkle over a little paprika and serve.

**BREAKFAST & BREADS**

# FETA WITH OLIVE OIL & ZA'ATAR

250g block of feta
3–4 tsp za'atar
2 tbsp olive oil

Place the feta on a plate. Mix together the za'atar and olive oil, and spoon over the top of the cheese.

# FETA WITH PISTACHIOS & DATE SYRUP

250g block of feta
2 tbsp date syrup
25g shelled pistachio
  nuts, toasted and
  chopped

Place the feta on a plate. Spoon the date syrup over the top of the cheese, then scatter over the pistachio nuts.

# FETA WITH SESAME SEEDS & HONEY

250g block of feta
1–2 tbsp runny honey
1 tsp toasted sesame
  seeds

Place the feta on a plate. Spoon the honey over the top of the cheese, then scatter over the sesame seeds.

My pitstop snack as a little boy when I ran in from playing with my friends was to wolf down a scrambled-egg sandwich – so quick and very filling. Then, later, as a teenager I loved merguez sausages – the spicier, the better – stuffed into a sandwich with frites (skinny, and sometimes not so skinny, hand-cut chips) and harissa. This recipe, inspired by my friend Aziz, who made it for me in Beirut, combines the two and uses Middle Eastern sujuk. It's thinner and longer than merguez, usually made from beef and flavoured with garlic, cumin and sumac. First make a big pan of scrambled eggs, then take it to another level by topping it with chunks of the sausage, just fried with some cherry tomatoes. A little pomegranate molasses and a sprinkling of parsley cuts through the richness. Use chorizo or merguez if you can't track down sujuk sausages.

# SUJUK SCRAMBLED EGGS
## BEYD BIL SUJUK

8 large eggs, beaten
1 tsp salt
a good grinding of black pepper
25g butter
2 tbsp chopped flat-leaf parsley
2 tsp olive oil
60g sujuk sausage, sliced into 1cm chunks
6 cherry tomatoes, halved
1 tbsp pomegranate molasses

Season the eggs with the salt and pepper and stir together. Heat the butter in a large frying pan over a low-to-medium heat. When the butter stops foaming, add the eggs. Start stirring the eggs to scramble them, watching them carefully. When they're half cooked, stir in half the parsley.

Keeping one eye on the eggs, cook the topping. Put a separate, smaller frying pan on a medium heat, add and heat the olive oil. Cook the sujuk chunks until golden and crisp, tossing regularly. Add the cherry tomatoes to the pan and cook until they've just blistered and turned golden on the flat side. Drizzle the pomegranate molasses over the top and toss everything again.

Check the eggs and stir them again – you want them to be cooked, but still a little soft. Spoon them into a bowl, then spoon the sujuk mixture on top. Drizzle over the juices and scatter over the remaining parsley, then serve.

SERVES 6

I love tartines, French open sandwiches, because I can see exactly what the filling is or, in this case, the topping. I've made this recipe a big, sharing crowd-pleasing affair, with cheese, honey, candied figs, nuts and fruit. For a slightly more decadent topping, swap the pomegranate seeds for dried rose petals and add just a drop of rose water to the syrup or honey before drizzling. If you prefer the feta uncooked to enjoy more of the salty flavour, sprinkle it on with the seeds and rose water just before eating. If you can't get hold of figs in syrup, poach dried figs in a little water to soften, then keep them in a jar with honey.

# FIG & FETA TARTINE

200g block of feta
1 large flatbread
2–3 tbsp fig syrup, or use honey if using dried figs
9 whole figs in syrup – or use dried figs – chopped into chunks
20g slivered or roughly chopped pistachio nuts
large handful of pomegranate seeds
1 tsp sesame seeds

Preheat the oven to 220°C/200°C fan/gas mark 7 and put a baking sheet in the oven to warm.

Put the feta into a bowl and mash it with a fork until it crumbles into small pieces.

Put the flatbread on a board and drizzle half the syrup over the top. Spoon the feta over the bread, covering it evenly. Then arrange the figs and pistachios over the top, again so they're evenly spaced on the bread.

Slide the flatbread on to the preheated baking sheet and bake in the oven for about 5 minutes – just long enough to warm the bread through and allow the feta to become very slightly golden. The bread shouldn't be too crisp.

Drizzle the remaining syrup over the top, followed by the pomegranate and sesame seeds. Cut into wedges and serve.

**SERVES 6**

If you're as greedy as me and like to pick at lots of bits, you'll love this. It's a true feast in every sense of the word and features lots of different dishes laid out in one big spread. This breakfast varies from family to family, village to village. For starters, you'll always find a selection of homemade cheese, eggs and flatbreads with different toppings. There'll also be jars of homemade jams such as quince, fig or rose petal. Olives and pickles, tomatoes, bunches of mint, baby cucumbers and radishes will be arranged in separate bowls. There'll always be space for labneh, of course – whether the topping is sweet or savoury depends on preference. And finally there'll be fresh fruit, whatever's in season. Here's a round-up of some of my favourites (see photos on pages 30-1).

# LEBANESE VILLAGE BREAKFAST
## FOTOOR ARABY

### LABNEH

Serve it plain or dressed as in the recipe on page 58. Or top it with something sweet - rose petal or quince jam are two of my favourites - or choose whatever you have to hand. It's also delicious with poached quinces and dried fruits (see page 40).

Labneh balls: serve as many different flavours as you like. There are plain labneh balls (dressed in a little olive oil), za'atar labneh balls, sumac labneh balls, labneh balls with flaked chilli, dried-mint labneh balls and labneh balls with nigella seeds.

### OLIVES & PICKLES

Green olives mixed with Kalamata olives, dressed in oil.

Whole green chillies, pickled turnips with beetroot and strips of Lebanese gherkins.

### FALAFEL

Serve plain and simple or try the recipe on page 82.

## A BOWL OF CRISP VEGETABLES

Slice baby cucumbers lengthways and sprinkle with a little salt

Carrots, squeezed with a little lemon juice and salt

Cherry tomatoes, halved, or large tomatoes, cut into wedges and opened like a flower, sprinkled with salt and sumac, and drizzled with a little olive oil

Radishes

Small bunch of mint, to garnish

## BREAD

Choose Arabic Bread (see page 51), Sesame Seed Bread (see page 50), Village Bread, or Man'ousha – either Spiced Tomato (see page 48) or Feta & Spinach (see page 49).

## EGGS

Hard-boiled eggs, halved, some sprinkled with za'atar and sumac, are the easiest to serve to a crowd. But if you fancy whipping up some scrambled eggs, serve them with feta and za'atar. If you're making fried eggs, do as I do and serve them out of the pan with a sprinkle of sumac on top.

## CHEESE

Grill slices of halloumi and serve with figs in rose syrup or roasted tomatoes (see page 102) or serve one or two of the Feta 4 Ways ideas on page 24.

And, finally, just to please some of my family, who love croissants for breakfast, I also like to serve a plate of the mini ones with my own Middle Eastern twist. I take half of them and split them, then drizzle over a little extra-virgin olive oil and za'atar. The other half I split and fill with salty feta and slices of juicy ripe tomatoes.

Originally from Egypt and made from beans in a simple vegetable sauce, this used to be known as the poor man's breakfast, but how times have changed. It's now seen as one of the healthiest ways to start the day and, in fact, I eat it particularly when I'm on a strict diet, training for a marathon.

It has to be made with fava beans, known as broad beans here, which have been dried then rehydrated. The onion and tomato sauce comes with a kick of garlic and spice, then is simmered with the beans until it forms a stew. If you stir the mixture a lot, the beans cook down and become very soft. I like it both ways – when the beans stay whole and have more texture or when they are more stewed, especially when served with a fried egg on top. Then I'll always add a drizzle of extra-virgin olive oil before tucking in.

# BROAD BEANS IN A TOMATO SAUCE
## FUL MEDAMES

1 tbsp extra-virgin olive oil, plus extra to drizzle
½ onion, chopped
2 garlic cloves, chopped
1 tsp cumin
2 large tomatoes, chopped, plus extra to garnish
½ tsp salt
400g tin ful medames (fava beans), drained
100–150ml water
small handful of coriander, chopped
1 spring onion, thinly sliced
bread, to serve

Heat the oil in a medium saucepan and stir in the onion. Sauté over a low-to-medium heat for 8-10 minutes until it has softened and turned golden.

Stir in the garlic and cumin, and cook for 1-2 minutes until you can smell the aroma as they cook in the heat of the pan.

Add the tomatoes, salt and beans with the water, then stir everything again. Simmer for a further 10 minutes, over a low-to-medium heat, until everything has cooked down and thickened, and the mixture looks like a stew.

Stir in most of the coriander and cook for a minute or two more to allow the herb to cook into the sauce. Check the seasoning. Spoon into a bowl and scatter over the remaining coriander, some chopped fresh tomatoes, the spring onions and a drizzle of olive oil over the top. Serve with bread.

SERVES 4-6

This is from my mum's very good Syrian friend, Soha (who we called Um Hassan), who came to our home town, Tizi Ouzou, to teach Arabic. She loved Algerian food, so my mum would invite her and her husband to eat with us. In return she also cooked for us, and this was one of her star dishes. Of course I ensured that my mum learnt how to make it, too. Now, our Syrian chef, Wassim, makes it in just the same way. I know some of you won't perhaps have tried lamb for breakfast, but it really works. Small pieces of lamb are seasoned with some of our favourite Middle Eastern spices, then cooked with courgettes and eggs. It's worth looking out for baby courgettes to use here, rather than their full-blown cousins, as they stay lovely and tender to the end.

# SCRAMBLED EGGS WITH LAMB & COURGETTES MOUFARAKET KOUSSA

100ml vegetable oil or
    100g ghee
1 onion, chopped
3 garlic cloves, sliced
150–200g lean lamb,
    chopped into very small
    pieces
1 tsp cinnamon
1 tsp Lebanese seven-
    spice mix
1 tsp allspice
1kg baby courgettes,
    chopped
125ml water
4 large eggs, beaten
2 tsp salt
1 tsp black pepper

TO SERVE
pinch of paprika
extra-virgin olive oil,
    to drizzle

Heat the oil or ghee in a large saucepan and sauté the onion and garlic for about 5 minutes until starting to soften.

Stir the lamb into the onion mixture and cook for about 1 minute, until starting to colour a little. Stir in the spices and cook for about 1 minute, then add the chopped courgette and the water, and mix everything together.

Cook, uncovered, over a medium heat for about 10 minutes, until the water has all been absorbed into the courgettes and they are tender.

Use a spoon to make a large hole in the middle of the courgettes. Add the eggs and the seasoning, and mix everything together.

Cover the pan with a lid and leave on the heat for about 1 minute until the eggs are cooked. Sprinkle with paprika and serve with a drizzle of extra-virgin olive oil.

SERVES 4–6

Here's a really great wrap that's quick to make and delicious. It's great for breakfast or brunch and has the added bonus that you can wrap it up and take it anywhere. Creamy labneh is spread over a flatbread, then topped with caramelised bananas. If you're going to take it with you, I'd skip that stage and just top it with some fresh fruit — my favourites are figs and strawberries or, of course, fresh banana. But the one ingredient I always make sure to add to the honey is plenty of orange blossom water or rose water, then I sprinkle the wrap with toasted sesame seeds at the end.

# LABNEH & CARAMELISED BANANA WRAP

50g butter
3 tbsp caster sugar
4 large bananas, sliced
6 flatbreads
200g labneh
6 tbsp runny honey, plus
    extra to drizzle
1–2 tbsp orange blossom
    water or rose water
plenty of toasted sesame
    seeds, to sprinkle

Heat a large frying pan over a medium heat and put the butter in the pan to melt. As soon as it has completely melted and stopped foaming, sprinkle over the caster sugar. Carefully lay the pieces of sliced banana over the base of the pan and cook until golden on each side, turning them after 1–2 minutes.

Lay the flatbreads on a board. Spread each one with an equal amount of labneh, leaving about 1cm border from the edge. Top with the caramelised slices of banana. Keep a few to one side (two or three per wrap is plenty) to garnish at the end.

Mix the honey with orange blossom water, then drizzle over each flatbread. Sprinkle over the sesame seeds, roll up and pop a couple of slices of banana on top of each to serve. I like it with an extra drizzle of honey and more sesame seeds over the top.

**SERVES 6**

I now realise how lucky I was as a little boy, being able to pick fruit straight from the tree. Quinces were one of the many fruits – along with pomegranates and figs – that I loved to gather then eat as soon as I got home. Although quinces are often cooked, they can be eaten raw in the Mediterranean and Middle East. We also cook them in a tagine, or roast halves until golden and tender, or poach them, as in this recipe. Make sure you buy dried figs, apricots and prunes, as opposed to the ready-to-eat fruit, as they'll be too soft once they've been cooked in the syrup. This keeps well in the fridge for up to a week if you don't eat it all at once.

# LABNEH WITH CARAMELISED POACHED QUINCES AND SPICED DRIED FRUIT LABNEH BIL SAFARJAL MESHWY

3 medium quinces
½ lemon
6 dried figs
6 dried apricots
6 dried prunes
40g sultanas
6 fresh or dried dates
2 cinnamon sticks
2 star anise
pared rind of 1 orange
juice of 2 oranges
150ml runny honey
200g caster sugar
500ml water
15g butter

TO SERVE
600g labneh or Greek
  yoghurt
zest of 1 orange
1 tbsp orange blossom
  water
1 tbsp toasted sesame
  seeds

Peel the quinces and cut them in half. Rub them with the half lemon, squeezing a little juice over them so the flesh doesn't turn brown. Put them in a large saucepan and add the figs, apricots, prunes and sultanas, followed by the dates, cinnamon sticks, star anise and orange rind. Next pour in the orange juice, honey, caster sugar and water.

Cover the pan with a lid and bring to the boil. Turn the heat down and simmer, covered, for 40–50 minutes or until the quinces have softened and turned pink.

Lift the quinces out, allowing any syrup to drip back into the pan. Put them on a plate. Melt the butter in a large frying pan over a low-to-medium heat and, as soon as it has stopped foaming, lay each quince half in the pan cut-side down and cook for a couple of minutes until caramelised. The quince syrup will become quite dark; make sure it doesn't burn or it will taste bitter.

Spoon the labneh into a large bowl and add the orange zest and orange blossom water, then swirl everything together and divide among six shallow bowls. Arrange the poached fruit around the sides and spoon a quince half into the middle of each dish, drizzling a little extra juice over the fruit so it oozes into the yoghurt. Finally, scatter over the sesame seeds and serve.

SERVES 6

This sweet brioche bread stuffed with dates can be found anywhere in the Middle East and is a particular favourite as my mum used to make it for us. It would be sliced, warm from the oven, for when we got home from school to eat with café crème (just like a latte). If I ever had a craving for it but couldn't make it I'd squash dates into bread to make a sandwich. Not quite the same, but you get the idea.

I like to be really generous with the dates, so there's a good balance between the soft brioche-style dough and the orange-scented dates within. This makes four loaves; I often serve it to friends, then give them half or a whole one to take away with them. (See photo on page 43.)

When you're cutting the dough before proving, make sure you slice all the way through to the middle and down the sides to reveal the date mixture. Once baked, I like to pull off these outer sections as an individual slice, then you're left with the middle to cut up.

# DATE BRIOCHE KAAK BIL TAMAR

1kg white bread flour,
    plus extra for rolling
2 tsp baking powder
300ml lukewarm water
100g granulated sugar
4 tsp dried yeast
3 large eggs, beaten
2 tsp salt
200ml sunflower oil
zest of 1 lemon or
    1 orange

FOR THE STUFFING & GLAZE
600g Medjool dates,
    pitted
3 tbsp orange blossom
    water
1 large egg, beaten
25g sesame seeds

Sieve the flour and baking powder into a large bowl and make a well in the centre. Pour the water into the middle, followed by the sugar, yeast and eggs.

Allow the yeast to activate - the mixture will become frothy after about 3–4 minutes - then pour into the flour mixture and mix well to make a soft dough.

Add the salt to the dough, along with the oil and lemon zest, and continue to mix and knead until the dough feels smooth and elastic. Transfer to a board when you feel it's ready to knead and work it until it's smooth.

Put into a clean bowl and cover, and leave to rise for 30 minutes, until it doubles in size.

Whizz the dates and orange blossom water together in a food processor to make a paste for the stuffing.

Divide the dough into four 450g pieces. Roll out each piece on a lightly floured board until it's a rough round measuring about 18cm across. Put a quarter of the date mixture in the middle and spread it out a little, leaving a border around the edges, then wrap the dough around the date mixture. Turn over so the seam is underneath. Repeat with the other three dough pieces, then set them aside to prove for 30 minutes.

Preheat the oven to 200°C/180°C fan/gas mark 6.

Flatten each loaf slightly and cut the edges to reveal the mixture inside, leaving a large ball in the middle.

Brush with some of the beaten egg and sprinkle with sesame seeds, then transfer to two lightly floured baking sheets and bake for about 35–40 minutes until the bread is dark golden. After about 20 minutes, glaze the loaves with the egg wash again and return to the oven to finish cooking.

Transfer to a wire rack to cool, then slice and serve.

**MAKES 4**

 **TONY'S TIP**

This is perfect to have alongside your afternoon coffee, or even served warm with a scoop of vanilla ice cream for pudding. If I'm feeling really indulgent I'll eat it with feta cheese, as the combination of salty feta and sweet dates is an absolute winner for me.

Man'eesh or man'ousha is to the Lebanese what pizza is to the Italians. You'll find it everywhere in the Middle East. Stuff it with mint, tomatoes, cucumber and pickles, then roll up into a sandwich, if you like. This recipe also works with gluten-free flour. (See photo on page 46.)

# SPICED TOMATO FLATBREADS
## MAN'OUSHA BANADORA BIL ZA'ATAR

### FOR THE DOUGH
1 tsp dried yeast
1 tsp caster sugar
100ml water
250g white bread flour
1 tbsp vegetable oil
50ml milk
½ tsp salt

### FOR THE TOPPING
2 tbsp extra-virgin olive oil
2 onions, finely chopped
1 garlic clove, crushed
2 tomatoes, finely chopped, plus extra to garnish
3 tbsp za'atar
small bunch of thyme, finely chopped
salt and black pepper

### TO SERVE
1 ripe tomato, finely chopped
few sprigs of thyme
toasted sesame seeds
extra-virgin olive oil, to drizzle

Put the yeast in a bowl and add a pinch of the sugar. Pour in half the water and set aside for 5 minutes to allow the yeast to activate.

Sift the flour into another bowl, make a well in the middle, add the yeast mixture, then the remaining sugar, the rest of the water, the oil, milk and salt. Stir together to make a dough, then knead on a board until smooth. Put in a clean bowl, cover and set aside to rise for 20–30 minutes.

To make the topping, heat the oil in a medium saucepan and cook the onions over a low heat for 10–15 minutes, until softened. Stir in the garlic, season well and cook for 1–2 minutes. Add the tomatoes and cook for about 10 minutes until they have broken down and softened, and the mixture looks juicy. Add the za'atar and thyme, increase the heat a little and cook for 3–5 minutes to thicken slightly.

Preheat the oven to its highest setting; it needs to be very hot. If you have a pizza stone, put it in now. Or use two large baking sheets.

Next, shape the dough. Divide it into three pieces and roll each piece into a round. To create a pattern round the edge, crimp the dough using your thumb and forefinger, holding a little bit of the outside edge and pushing into the dough with the forefinger of the opposite hand to create a pattern. Do this all the way round, then crimp the edges on the two other rounds of dough.

Once the pizza stone or baking sheets are hot, slide the dough on to them. Spoon the tomato mixture on top, spreading it out to the side, then bake in the oven for 7–10 minutes until the bread is golden.

Once cooked, slide the flatbreads onto a board. Scatter over the chopped tomato, thyme and sesame seeds, and drizzle with olive oil.

**SERVES 6**

This man'ousha, topped with spinach and feta, is a recipe given to us by the mother of Firas, one of the Syrian chefs who bakes and makes patisserie for us. Once I tasted it, I just had to put it on the menu, so we added it the very next day. (See photo on page 47.)

# FETA & SPINACH FLATBREADS
## MAN'OUSHA SABANEGH WA JABNAT AL FETA

FOR THE DOUGH
1 tsp dried yeast
1 tsp caster sugar
100ml lukewarm water
250g white bread flour
1 tbsp vegetable oil
50ml milk
½ tsp salt

FOR THE TOPPING
2 tbsp olive oil
1 small onion, finely
  chopped
1 garlic clove, crushed
pinch of sumac, plus
  extra to sprinkle over
  at the end
400g spinach leaves
1 lemon, halved
75g feta, crumbled
30g pine nuts
salt and black pepper

TO SERVE
small handful of fresh
  pomegranate seeds
small handful of mint
  leaves
pomegranate molasses,
  to drizzle
extra-virgin olive oil, to
  drizzle

Put the yeast in a bowl and add a pinch of the sugar. Pour in half the water and set aside for 5 minutes to allow the yeast to activate.

Sift the flour into another bowl, make a well in the middle, add the yeast mixture, then the remaining sugar, the rest of the water, the oil, milk and salt. Stir together to make a dough, then knead on a board until smooth. Put in a clean bowl, cover and set aside to rise for 20–30 minutes.

To make the topping, heat the oil in a medium frying pan and cook the onion over a low heat for 10-15 minutes until softened. Stir in the garlic, season well with salt, pepper and the sumac, and cook for 1–2 minutes more. Add the spinach to the pan and squeeze in the juice of half the lemon. Cook for a couple of minutes more, stirring the spinach around in the pan so that it wilts in the heat. Rest a sieve over a bowl, spoon the mixture into it and allow it to drain. This ensures that the man'ousha will not end up soggy.

Preheat the oven to its highest setting; it needs to be very hot. If you have a pizza stone, put it in now. Or use two large baking sheets.

Next, shape the dough. Divide the dough into three pieces and roll each piece into a round. Once the pizza stone or baking sheets are hot, slide the pieces of dough on to them. Spoon the spinach mixture on top, spreading it out to the side, then scatter over the feta and pine nuts. Bake in the oven for 7-10 minutes until the bread is golden.

Once the flatbreads are cooked, slide them on to a board. Scatter over the pomegranate seeds and mint, and sprinkle with sumac. Drizzle over the molasses and extra-virgin olive oil. Squeeze over a little more lemon juice and serve.

**SERVES 6**

'Kaak' in Arabic means 'bread', and these, with their distinctive handbag shape, are at their best fresh from the oven. Topped with sesame seeds, they are thinner than other breads, but you can prise them open and fill them with anything – salty feta and slices of juicy ripe tomatoes are always good in my book. You can see the shape in the photo on page 50.

# SESAME SEED BREAD
## KAAK BIL SEMSSOUM

150ml tepid water
12–15g dried yeast
50g sugar
500g white bread flour,
 plus extra for rolling
10g salt
1 medium egg
100ml vegetable oil, plus
 extra for greasing
sesame seeds, to
 sprinkle

FOR THE EGG WASH
2 medium eggs
1 tsp white wine vinegar

Pour half the water into a bowl and sprinkle over the yeast. Add a pinch of the sugar and stir everything together. Set aside to allow the yeast to activate for 5 minutes.

Sift the flour into a large bowl and stir in the rest of the sugar and the salt. Make a well in the middle and add the egg and oil. Whisk the egg to break it down. Pour the yeast mixture into the middle, rinsing out the bowl with a little of the remaining water so that all the yeast goes in. Pour the rest of the water into the flour mixture.

Mix all the ingredients together to make a rough dough, then tip it on to a board and knead well until it's really smooth. This will take about 5–10 minutes. Put into a clean bowl, cover and leave in a warm place for about 40 minutes.

Divide the dough into six equal pieces. Take each piece and roll it in the palm of your hand to make a ball.

Lightly flour the work surface and roll out one piece until it measures about ½cm thick and about 15cm across. Use a 5-cm round cutter to cut out a circle at the top, near the edge on one side of the round. Pull this bit of dough out to make a handbag shape.

**TONY'S TIP**

You can bake the small rounds of dough you've cut out to make little rolls. Brush with the egg wash, scatter over the sesame seeds and put them on a separate tray. Bake them for about 10–12 minutes.

Beat the eggs and white wine vinegar together in a bowl. Brush this all over the dough, then spread liberally with sesame seeds, pressing them down so that they stick to the egg wash. Slide on to a lightly oiled baking sheet (or lined with baking parchment). Do the same with the rest of the dough until you've made six breads in total. Put to one side at room temperature for 40–50 minutes.

Preheat the oven to 200°C/180°C fan/gas mark 6. Transfer the baking sheets to the oven and bake for 15–20 minutes until golden.

MAKES 6

BREAKFAST & BREADS

You'll never see an Arabic table without bread on it. Bread means so much to people in the Middle East that if we don't have any bread, we wonder how can we eat the food – there's nothing to dip into the sauces or mop up any juices from a stew. Sometimes I have wondered whether the food that's served is more important or the bread. That's why I'm keen to share my pitta bread recipe so you, too, can always serve bread. This recipe has a particularly wholesome taste, thanks to the wholmeal flour, and is scattered with nigella seeds before baking for extra flavour.

# ARABIC BREAD KHOBZ

1 tsp dried yeast
10g sugar
220ml lukewarm water
300g white bread flour
100g brown bread flour
5g salt
2 tsp olive oil
nigella seeds, to sprinkle

Put the yeast into a bowl with a good pinch of the sugar and half the water. Set aside for 5 minutes to allow the yeast to activate and become frothy.

Sieve the flours into a large bowl and stir in the salt. Make a well in the middle and pour in the oil, the yeast mixture and the remaining sugar and water. Stir everything together to make a rough dough. Knead on a board until smooth.

Put the dough into a clean bowl, cover and leave to rise for about 30 minutes until doubled in size.

Divide the dough into 12 pieces and roll them into rounds on a lightly floured surface. Sprinkle a few nigella seeds over the top of each piece before the final roll so they stick to the surface on the final roll. Put the pieces of rolled dough on to floured baking sheets and cover. Leave in a warm place for 45 minutes–1 hour to prove.

Preheat the oven to its hottest temperature.

Bake the pitta breads for 4–5 minutes until the dough has puffed up slightly and is cooked all the way through.

**MAKES 12**

No Middle Eastern meal is complete without some mezze. The more mezze on the table the happier I become and if I'm feasting with friends and family there will be so much food you won't be able to see the table!

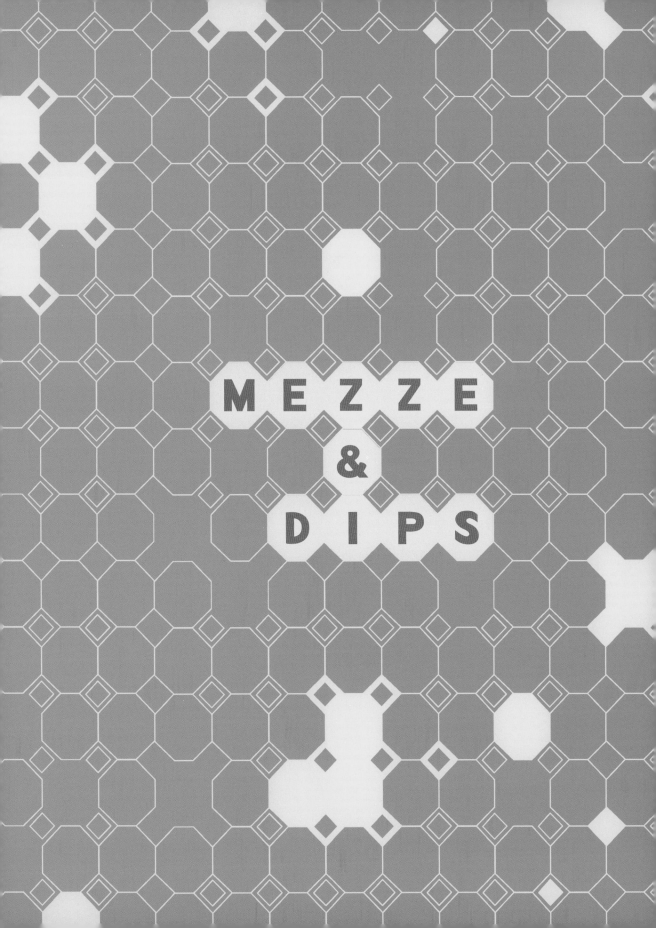

# MEZZE & DIPS

HOMMOS 4 WAYS

I love hommos with a creamy texture and packed with garlic and tahina. I'm even happier if it's served drizzled with peppery olive oil and flatbread to dip in. (See photos on pages 54–5.)

This recipe calls for dried chickpeas. When you cook them yourself, you can check when they are ready. I test by pressing one between finger and thumb – it should easily squash into a paste. Too hard and they won't whizz into a smooth mixture; too soft and the texture won't be right.

And, yes, that's right, there are ice cubes in the ingredients list! Don't add water instead as it will make the finished texture too watery.

# CLASSIC HOMMOS

125g dried chickpeas
¾ tsp bicarbonate of
soda
3–4 ice cubes
35–50g tahina
juice of ½ lemon
1 small garlic clove,
crushed (optional)
½ tsp salt

The night before you want to make the hommos, put the chickpeas into a bowl and cover them with cold water. Set aside and leave to soak for at least 8-10 hours.

The next day, drain the chickpeas and return to the bowl. Add the bicarbonate of soda and cover with cold water. Soak for 30 minutes.

Drain off the water again and put the chickpeas into a medium saucepan. Pour in enough cold water to cover them by a couple of centimetres, then put a lid on the pan and bring to the boil.

Skim all the scum from the top as it comes to the boil, then half cover the pan and simmer gently for 40-45 minutes until you can easily squeeze a chickpea between your finger and thumb. Make sure the water doesn't boil so the chickpeas don't break up.

As soon as they're done, drain the chickpeas and cool until just warm. Tip into a food processor with the ice and blend until smooth. This will take a couple of minutes and the mixture will turn from chickpea yellow to pale and creamy. Add the tahina and blend again, then finally, blend with the lemon juice, garlic (if using) and salt.

Taste to check the seasoning and serve.

**SERVES 4–6**

## HOMMOS BEIRUTY

Once the chickpeas are cooked, set aside a large spoonful to stir in at the end. Make the hommos with the remaining chickpeas, following the classic recipe, then transfer to a bowl and stir in 1 crushed garlic clove, ½–1 chopped and deseeded red or green chilli, a small handful of finely chopped flat-leaf parsley and the reserved whole chickpeas. Spoon into another bowl and serve.

∧∧∧∧∧∧∧∧∧∧∧∧

## BEETROOT HOMMOS

Make the hommos following the classic recipe and leave the hommos in the food processor. Grate 150g cooked beetroot and add most of it to the food processor. Whizz until smooth. Transfer into a bowl, then spoon the remaining grated beetroot into the middle, sprinkle with sumac and serve.

∧∧∧∧∧∧∧∧∧∧∧∧

## RED PEPPER HOMMOS

Make the hommos following the classic recipe and leave it in the food processor. Slice 2 red peppers in half and put on a baking sheet. Grill under a hot grill until the skins blister and blacken. Put in a bowl, cover and leave for about 10 minutes for the skin to steam off. Remove and discard the cores and skins, then finely chop the flesh. Set aside about a quarter and add the remaining chopped pepper to the food processor. Whizz until smooth. Transfer to a bowl, then spoon the remaining chopped pepper into the middle, sprinkle over a few chilli flakes and serve.

∧∧∧∧∧∧∧∧∧∧∧∧

## HOMMOS WITH LAMB & PINE NUTS

Make the hommos following the classic recipe. Heat 1 tablespoon of olive oil in a saucepan and sauté ½ chopped onion for about 8 minutes over a medium heat until starting to turn golden. Stir in 1 crushed garlic clove and cook for 1 minute. Add 100g lamb mince, a pinch each of cinnamon, Lebanese seven-spice mix and allspice, and season with salt and black pepper. Cook, stirring occasionally, until it's golden and cooked through, and the mixture looks crumbled. Spoon the hommos into a bowl and top with the mince mixture, 1 deseeded and finely chopped tomato, 15g toasted pine nuts, 2 teaspoons paprika and a small handful of chopped flat-leaf parsley to garnish.

Labneh takes time to make from scratch as it's produced by straining creamy yoghurt through a clean muslin cloth to drain away the whey. The resulting solids resemble a smooth, creamy cheese and have a rich taste.

There are some very good ready-made versions available and – I'll let you into a secret – it tastes just like cream cheese, so buy that if you can't find the traditional one. All that's required for this dip is to beat labneh with mint, spring onions and cherry tomatoes, then spoon it into a bowl and drizzle with a little oil to serve. The super-fresh flavours are a perfect match for hot crisp-skinned pitta.

# LABNEH DIP

5g fresh mint
300g labneh
1 tsp salt
2 spring onions, finely chopped
5 cherry tomatoes, each cut into 8 pieces

TO SERVE
extra-virgin olive oil
sprigs of mint
2–3 cherry tomatoes, quartered

Pull the mint leaves off the sprigs and chop finely. Place in a small mixing bowl and spoon in the labneh, salt, spring onions and cherry tomatoes.

Beat all the ingredients together until the juice bursts from the tomatoes and everything is mixed well.

Spoon into a small bowl and use the back of a spoon to make a hollow in the middle. Drizzle a little olive oil into the hollow, then arrange a few mint leaves around the outside, alongside the tomato quarters.

SERVES 6

You may recognise this as being similar to Baba Ghanuj – and you're right, it is, the main difference being that this is given extra flavour and texture by the walnuts that are stirred in.

When you're choosing the aubergines for this, pick them up and weigh them in your hands. They should feel heavy and should also have smooth, shiny skins and fresh-looking green stalks. The grilling is important, too. The skin needs to be very black on the outside – not just a different shade of aubergine – for the inside to be thoroughly cooked. That way the texture of the dip will be smooth and easy to mix with the other ingredients in the finished dip (see photo on page 61). If I'm being healthy, I like to serve it with Little Gem lettuce leaves and cucumber or carrot sticks.

# AUBERGINE & WALNUT DIP BABA BIL JOZ

2 medium aubergines
40g tahina
60g Greek yoghurt or
   labneh
7g chopped walnuts
1 garlic clove, grated
5–7g chopped dill, plus
   extra to serve
1 tsp salt

TO SERVE
extra-virgin olive oil
5–6 walnut quarters and
   halves
sumac, to sprinkle
1 Little Gem lettuce,
   leaves separated

Start by preparing the aubergines. Preheat the grill until really hot, then put the aubergines on a baking sheet and grill until the skin has blackened and blistered. You'll need to turn them regularly as it's important that the flesh inside is really well-cooked.

Cool the aubergines a little, then peel away and discard the skin. Chop the flesh coarsely, then scrape it into a bowl. Add the remaining ingredients and beat well to make a smooth dip. Check the seasoning and spoon into a bowl.

Take the back of a spoon and make a big swirl in the dip. Drizzle with a little oil, garnish with the extra chopped dill, the walnut halves and some sumac – sprinkle it generously, all round the edge. Serve with the Little Gem leaves to scoop up the dip.

SERVES 6

This lovely creamy concoction reminds me of when the smell of frying would lure me into the kitchen as a little boy. I'd stand next to my mum by the hob, and she'd be turning the coin-sized slices of courgette in a frying pan until they were golden. Seasoned with a little salt, some crushed garlic and a few drops of lemon juice, we'd enjoy them by the plateful.

This recipe, which sautés the courgettes until tender, then mixes them with tahina, is one of our favourite dishes in the restaurant, where we serve it with warm, freshly made pitta bread. We garnish it with crisp strings of deep-fried courgette (see photo on page 61) – I particularly love the texture combination of the crunchy courgettes on top of the smooth pitta bread. See below for my tip on how to do it.

# COURGETTE & TAHINA DIP
## KOOSA BIL TAHINA

3 tbsp olive oil
500g courgettes, trimmed and chopped into 1–2cm cubes
50g tahina
150g Greek yoghurt
50g mint sprigs
1 tsp salt
¼ tsp black pepper
½ tsp cumin

Heat the oil in a large sauté pan and add the chopped courgettes. Cover the pan with a lid and fry over a low heat for 12–15 minutes until the courgettes are very soft. Toss them every now and then so that they cook evenly and don't stick to the base of the pan.

Cool a little, then put into a food processor. Add the tahina and yoghurt. Pull the leaves from the mint sprigs (discard the tough stalks) and put them into a food processor with the salt, pepper and cumin. Blitz to make a smooth purée.

Taste to adjust the seasoning, then spoon into a bowl and serve.

**SERVES 6**

**TONY'S TIP**

Finely slice ½ small courgette into thin strips and fry in a little olive oil until golden and crisp. Spoon on top of the dip and garnish it with small fresh mint leaves and a good pinch of cumin seeds over the top and around the edge of the dip, then finish with a little extra-virgin olive oil.

MEZZE & DIPS

There were always lots of fresh ingredients around when I was growing up, and whenever my mum or dad brought fresh broad beans home from the market, I'd sneak into the kitchen to steal a handful. Popping them from the pod, peeling them, then savouring the sweet taste was the best part.

The bright green hue and silky texture of this dip never fails to make me smile (see photo on page 65). It's rich, thanks to the tahina, but very healthy when served with lots of crudités. Take care to add the water slowly, or the finished mixture can end up more of a purée than a thick dip.

# BROAD BEAN & TAHINA DIP FOOLYAH

300g frozen broad
  beans, thawed
handful of ice cubes, for
  cooling
75ml water or a few ice
  cubes
90g tahina
2 garlic cloves, grated
juice of 1 lemon
½ tbsp salt
1 tbsp cumin
extra-virgin olive oil,
  to serve
sumac, to serve

Bring a large saucepan of water to the boil. While the water's heating, slip the skins off the broad beans and discard them. Put the handful of ice cubes into a bowl, then add enough water to fill it half full.

When the water in the pan is boiling, drop the broad beans in and cook for 1 minute. Drain well, then spoon them into the bowl of iced water to cool down quickly. Drain again, set aside a spoonful of broad beans to garnish the dip at the end, then transfer the remaining beans to the bowl of a food processor.

Pour the water into the food processor, or add the ice cubes, and blitz until smooth. Add the tahina, garlic, lemon juice, salt and cumin, and whizz again to incorporate these ingredients. Spoon into a bowl, top with the reserved broad beans, a drizzle of oil and a pinch of sumac.

**SERVES 6–8**

MEZZE & DIPS

From early summer to late autumn you'll find fresh globe artichokes in the shops. I love them when they've been boiled until tender, then dipping the leaves into peppery extra-virgin olive oil mixed with a little fresh garlic and lemon juice.

This recipe calls for artichoke hearts so I've taken a short cut and used a tin instead. First they're roasted with garlic at a high temperature to enhance the flavour, then they're blitzed with our other favourite flavourings – lemon, fresh coriander and cumin. The dip is then finished with tahina to add richness and more flavour (see photo on page 65).

# ARTICHOKE HEART & TAHINA DIP
## KHARSHOOF BIL TAHINA

250g tinned artichoke
  hearts, drained
3 garlic cloves
1 tbsp olive oil
juice of 1 lemon
small handful of chopped
  coriander, plus extra to
  garnish
½ tbsp salt
1 tbsp cumin
80g tahina

Preheat the oven to 220°C/200°C fan/gas mark 7.

Chop the artichoke hearts into quarters and put into a bowl. Add the garlic. Pour over the oil. Toss well so that everything is coated in the oil, then put in a small roasting tin and roast for 8–10 minutes, until starting to turn golden.

Leave the artichokes to cool a little, then spoon them into the bowl of a food processor. Squeeze the purée out of the garlic cloves into the bowl, too.

Add all the remaining ingredients and blitz until smooth. If the texture is still quite chunky, add a couple of ice cubes and blitz again until smooth. Taste to check the seasoning and garnish with the extra coriander.

**SERVES 6–8**

I had to include this recipe as it makes me think of when I was a boy and my foot became infected. My mum fried some onions with the intention of bandaging them around the swelling, but as soon as I smelled the gorgeous cooking aroma, I said, 'Before you do anything, please make me a fried onion sandwich.' This has a few more colourful vegetables thrown in.

# FRIED VEGETABLES WITH YOGHURT & TAHINA SAUCE MAKALEE KHODAR

2 aubergines, chopped into 2cm cubes

1 whole cauliflower, chopped into even-sized florets

2 red and 2 green peppers, halved, deseeded and chopped into 3cm cubes

3 large courgettes, sliced

2–3 whole red chillies (optional)

sunflower oil, for deep-frying

salt, for sprinkling

FOR THE SAUCE

220g Greek or natural yoghurt

80g tahina

1 garlic clove, crushed

generous handful of flat-leaf parsley, chopped – I like to see the green in the sauce

TO SERVE

small mint leaves

lemon wedges

Preheat the oven to 100°C/80°C fan/gas mark ¼, then prepare all of the vegetables.

Heat the oil in a deep-fat fryer (or use a large, deep saucepan) until the temperature reaches 190°C or a cube of bread sizzles madly in the hot oil.

Deep-fry the vegetables in batches until golden and cooked through, then drain on kitchen paper and sprinkle with salt. Transfer to the oven to keep warm.

Once all the vegetables are fried, make the sauce by stirring the yoghurt, tahina, garlic and parsley together in a bowl. If it's too thick, loosen it with a couple of spoonfuls of water. Serve alongside the vegetables with extra mint leaves and lemon wedges to squeeze over.

SERVES 6–8

 TONY'S TIP

I've suggested preparing enough vegetables to cover a whole platter, but if you don't manage to eat them all, they'll keep well in the fridge for up to 5 days, stored in a sealed container. I also love to eat them squashed into pitta or a wrap, first smeared with a little spicy hommos and topped with crumbled feta and a splash of olive oil.

Our Syrian chef, Wassim, introduced me to this dip, which I loved instantly. It's a simple one-pan recipe, in which red peppers are cooked with chillies, onion, garlic and spices until they're soft and silky, then lots of chopped roasted nuts are stirred in at the end to give it texture. It's a perfect marriage of ingredients for me. Depending on the strength of your fresh chillies, this dish ranges from mildly spiced to very hot. If you prefer it less spicy, go easy on the chilli flakes, too. Start by adding a quarter of a teaspoon, then work up until you reach the required level.

# ALEPPO ROAST PEPPERS & MIXED NUT DIP MUHAMARA HALLABYAH

3–4 tbsp olive oil
1 tsp nigella seeds
2 red peppers, halved, deseeded and finely chopped
2 red chillies, halved, deseeded and finely chopped, plus extra, sliced, to garnish
½ onion, finely chopped
2 garlic cloves, finely chopped
2 tsp cumin
2 tsp paprika
1 tsp chilli flakes
1 tsp salt
3 vine tomatoes, finely chopped
2 tbsp pomegranate molasses
200g roasted mixed nuts, chopped

TO SERVE
1–2 tsp slivered pistachio nuts

Heat a drizzle of the oil in a sauté pan and fry the nigella seeds for 1–2 minutes. Scoop out and set aside.

Add the remaining oil to the pan then the peppers, chillies, onion and garlic, and cook over a low heat for 10 minutes. Stir regularly so that it all cooks evenly.

Stir in the cumin, paprika, chilli flakes, toasted nigella seeds and salt, and continue to cook for 1–2 minutes. Then stir in the tomatoes and cook for a further 10 minutes, still on a low heat. Set aside to cool.

Stir in the pomegranate molasses and the nuts, then spoon into a bowl and make a dip in the middle. Garnish the area around the dip with sliced chilli, then spoon the slivered pistachios inside.

SERVES 6

### TONY'S TIP

If you want to roast the mixed nuts yourself, here's how to do it. Preheat the oven to 220°C/200°C fan/gas mark 7. Tip the nuts on to a baking tray and spread them out in an even layer. Roast for 6–8 minutes, tossing half way through, until golden.

Meat was scarce when I was younger and we ate it perhaps once a week or fortnight. Instead, potatoes formed the base of many meals. They're chunky and filling, and whether in a stew, or served with a minted herb and tomato sauce, or fried with an egg – or even stuffed into a sandwich – they'd be delicious.

This warm mezze has an equal balance between potatoes and vegetables, and really will please everyone, whether they're vegan, vegetarian or a die-hard carnivore. Chunks of bite-size vegetables are fried until just tender, then tossed in a spicy pepper sauce, followed by a handful of fresh coriander thrown in to wilt at the end. Of course, it can be served as part of a larger selection of dishes, but I find a warm bowlful served on its own just as satisfying.

# SPICED POTATOES BATATA HARRA

vegetable or sunflower
  oil, for deep-frying
1 large potato, cubed
1 large aubergine, cubed
2 courgettes, cubed
1 red pepper, deseeded
  and cubed
1 green pepper, deseeded
  and cubed
½ tsp cumin

FOR THE SAUCE
3 tbsp olive oil
1 red and 1 green pepper,
  halved, deseeded and
  finely chopped
1 green and 1 red chilli,
  halved, deseeded and
  finely chopped
4 garlic cloves, chopped
small handful of
  coriander, roughly
  chopped
salt and black pepper

Start by making the sauce. Heat the oil in a frying pan and sauté the peppers, chillies and garlic for 10-15 minutes until softened. Stir in the coriander and season.

Meanwhile, heat the oil in a deep-fat fryer or a deep saucepan until hot (about 190°C). Fry the vegetables in batches until golden, draining them on kitchen paper as each batch is cooked.

Transfer to a large bowl and spoon the sauce over the top. Add the cumin, salt and coriander, and mix everything together very gently so the vegetables aren't crushed.

SERVES 6

When I was growing up in my home town of Tizi Ouzou buying a chicken was very different to the way we'd buy one today. Dad would go to a shop that sold live birds and choose the best one, which would then be slaughtered and cleaned in front of him. Mum would cook it, and we would fight over the best bits. As the eldest I often managed to win, so the wings are very special to me. This recipe uses lots of oil, lemon juice and garlic, and the flavours are so powerful, so moreish, I make it again and again.

# MARINATED CHICKEN WINGS JAWANEH

2 tbsp olive oil
2 tbsp cider vinegar
1 tsp salt
juice of 1½ large lemons
2 garlic cloves, crushed
1–2 pinches cinnamon
1–2 pinches cardamom
small bunch of coriander
500g chicken wings
1 lemon, cut into
  wedges, to serve

Preheat the oven to 100°C/80°C fan/gas mark ¼.

Put the oil, vinegar, salt, lemon juice, garlic, cinnamon and cardamom into a large, sealable container. Stir them together. Take half the coriander and chop it – not too finely, but not too coarsely either. Add this to the container, along with the chicken wings and use a large spoon to mix everything together so that the wings are covered in the marinade.

Cover the box and put in the fridge to marinate for at least 4 hours or, even better, overnight.

Take the wings out of the fridge about half an hour before you're going to cook them to take the chill off them.

Heat a large frying pan over a medium heat until medium hot. Lift the chicken wings out of the marinade and scrape any garlic back into the marinade – it'll be used to flavour the sauce later.

Place half the wings in the pan and fry for 5–7 minutes until sticky and golden on one side, then turn them over and cook the other side for the same length of time. You may need to prop them up on the side of the pan to make sure all the flesh cooks – check each one as you're cooking them. Put on a plate and keep warm in the oven. Once half are done, cook the other half and transfer them to the oven, too.

Pour the marinade into the frying pan, add 1–2 tablespoons of water and bring to a simmer. Cook for 1–2 minutes, scraping the base of the pan to lift the sticky juices and mix into the sauce. Add any juices from the rested chicken wings to the pan and stir them in. Chop the remaining coriander and stir in, too. Serve with lemon wedges.

**SERVES 6**

Squid is one of the many types of seafood I ate as a child – fried or grilled and seasoned with my favourite extra-virgin olive oil and lemon juice, it was very simple, yet utterly delicious. This recipe is slightly more involved, but the method – simple acts of blending, tossing and frying – means it's actually a bit of a cinch to make. The harissa provides the perfect backdrop to the crisp rings of subtly spiced squid.

# SPICED FRIED SQUID WITH HARISSA SAUCE HABAR MAKLEE

100g plain flour
1 tsp sumac
1 tsp cumin
1 tsp chilli powder
½ tsp salt, plus extra for sprinkling
400g frozen squid tubes, thawed
sunflower oil, for deep-frying

FOR THE HARISSA SAUCE
450g jar roasted red peppers in brine, drained
5 garlic cloves
4–5 red chillies, halved and deseeded
2 tbsp tomato purée
2 tbsp cider vinegar
2 tbsp vegetable oil
1 tsp cumin
1 tsp chilli powder
1 tsp black pepper
½ tsp salt
2 tbsp coconut milk
2 tbsp runny honey

Preheat the oven to 100°C/80°C fan/gas mark ¼.

Start by making the harissa. Put the drained peppers into the bowl of a food processor. Add the garlic, chillies, tomato purée, cider vinegar, vegetable oil, cumin, chilli powder, pepper and salt, and blitz. You could also do this in a large bowl, using a hand blender.

Add the coconut milk and runny honey, and blitz again. Set the bowl of harissa to one side while you prepare the squid.

Put the flour, sumac, cumin, chilli powder and salt into a large bowl and toss. Slice the squid into 1cm pieces and add to the flour mixture. Toss well to coat the rings with all the ingredients.

Heat the oil in a deep-fat fryer (or large, deep saucepan) until the temperature reaches 190°C or a cube of bread sizzles madly in it.

Fry the squid a handful at a time until golden. Drain on kitchen paper and sprinkle with salt. Transfer to an ovenproof dish and keep warm in the oven. Continue to deep-fry the squid in batches, keeping them warm as you do so, and serve with the sauce.

**SERVES 6–8**

### TONY'S TIP

The harissa recipe makes more than enough to serve with the squid, but it keeps well in the fridge. I find myself drizzling it over feta in a salad or just-griddled juicy lamb chops and sujuk or merguez sausages for a spicy kick.

The moreish, velvety texture of chicken livers are, for me, a winning combination served with soft grilled cherry tomatoes, slightly sharp pomegranate molasses and fragrant fresh coriander. This is a great mezze dish as part of a feast, or serve it simply with some flatbreads to scoop up all the rich-flavoured juices.

# CHICKEN LIVERS WITH CHERRY TOMATOES & POMEGRANATE MOLASSES KASBAT DOJOJ BIL DEBS EL ROMANE

1kg chicken livers
6 garlic cloves, crushed
1 cinnamon stick
1 tbsp salt
½ tsp black pepper
½ tsp Lebanese seven-
    spice mix
vegetable oil, to cover
4 tbsp olive oil, plus
    extra to fry the
    tomatoes
200g cherry tomatoes,
    halved
juice of 2 lemons
1 tsp pomegranate
    molasses
seeds of ½ pomegranate
20g fresh coriander
fried onion and garlic,
    to serve (optional, see
    Tony's tip)

Put the chicken livers in a deep frying pan and add 5 of the crushed garlic cloves and the cinnamon stick. Sprinkle over the salt, pepper and seven-spice mix, then pour enough vegetable oil over the top to just cover the livers.

Cover the pan with a lid and bring to a simmer. Turn the heat down low and allow the livers to braise slowly for 30 minutes. Drain the fat away and spoon the livers into a bowl.

Heat a little olive oil in a separate frying pan and quickly cook the cherry tomatoes until golden and softened.

Heat the olive oil in a third frying pan and quickly stir-fry the livers. Add the lemon juice and pomegranate molasses, and taste to check the seasoning. Season with salt and pepper if necessary. Spoon the tomatoes on top then divide among six plates. Scatter over the pomegranate seeds and coriander, and the fried onion and garlic, too, if you like.

**SERVES 6, GENEROUSLY**

### TONY'S TIP

In the restaurant, we deep-fry sliced onion and garlic to garnish this dish. If you want to do this at home, you can achieve a similar result by frying the onion over a low heat until it caramelises. Heat a couple of tablespoons of oil in a frying pan and cook ½ sliced onion over a medium heat until golden. Add 1–2 thinly sliced garlic cloves to the pan and cook until golden. Season with salt and spoon on top of the livers.

These little open pies are so moreish, I can never stop after just one. They are traditionally served as part of a mezze feast. They're so delicious, not just warm from the oven, but also cold, and you could even take them on a picnic.

# SPICED LAMB PASTRIES SFEEHA

### FOR THE DOUGH
500g strong plain flour, plus a little extra for rolling out
1 tsp fast-action dried yeast
1 tsp caster sugar
350–400ml warm water
½ teaspoon salt

### FOR THE FILLING
250g lamb mince
250g tomatoes, halved, deseeded and finely chopped
1 small onion, finely chopped
1 green chilli, halved, deseeded and finely chopped
1 tsp Lebanese seven-spice mix
½ tsp salt
black pepper
½ tsp cinnamon
75ml pomegranate molasses

### TO SERVE
pomegranate seeds
baby mint leaves
harissa sauce (see recipe on page 74)
tarator sauce (see recipe on page 119)

Start by making the dough. Sift the flour into a bowl, make a well in the middle and sprinkle in the yeast and caster sugar. Add the water, mix a little, then add the salt and mix everything together. Knead on a board for about 10 minutes. The dough should feel soft, sticky and smooth. Put in a bowl, cover and set aside for 30 minutes to give the dough time to double in size.

Mix all the filling ingredients together in a large bowl. Set aside. Preheat the oven to 200°C/180°C fan/gas mark 6.

Sprinkle a little flour over a clean work surface to roll out the dough. I find it easier to work with smaller pieces of dough as we're cutting out rounds to make the sfeeha. So chop the dough into about six even chunks. Take one piece and roll it out until it's about 5–7mm thick. Stamp out rounds using a 9cm cutter. Spoon a little lamb mince into the middle and spread it out, leaving a narrow border.

Use your thumb and forefinger to pinch two sides of the dough together to make a corner, then do this three more times at regular points to make a square. Transfer to an oiled baking sheet (or one lined with baking parchment) then continue to make the sfeeha until you've used up all the dough. You'll need two or three baking sheets, depending on how large they are.

Bake in the oven for 20 minutes until golden. Cool a little on a wire rack then serve scattered with the pomegranate seeds and mint leaves, alongside the two sauces.

**MAKES ABOUT 24**

 **TONY'S TIP**

If you want to get ahead, mix the filling the night before and store it in the fridge in a sealed container. Take it out once the dough has started to rise so it has a chance to come up to room temperature.

If you peeked inside some village homes, you'd find Lebanese mamas rustling up these little tasty parcels.

# PASTRIES STUFFED WITH FETA & HALLOUMI OR OLIVES SAMBOUSSEK

500g white flour, plus
  extra for rolling
20g sugar
1 tbsp salt
1 tbsp beaten egg plus 1
  large egg, beaten, for
  brushing
1 tbsp vegetable oil
15g butter, melted and
  cooled a little
250ml water

FOR THE CHEESE FILLING
125g halloumi, grated
125g feta, crumbled
½ tbsp nigella seeds,
  plus extra to garnish
3 spring onions, chopped
10g mint sprigs, leaves
  picked and chopped

FOR THE OLIVE FILLING
200g green olives and
  black Kalamata olives,
  stoned and chopped
10g thyme sprigs, leaves
  picked and chopped
½ tbsp red pepper paste
1 garlic clove, chopped
½ tsp black pepper
sesame seeds or nigella
  seeds, to garnish

Sift the flour into a large bowl and stir in the sugar and salt. Make a well in the middle and pour in the tablespoon of beaten egg, the oil, cool melted butter and water. Stir everything together to make a rough dough, then transfer to a board and knead until smooth. Set aside.

Mix the cheese filling ingredients in one bowl, and the olive filling ingredients in another.

Roll out the dough on a lightly floured board until it's about ½cm thick and use a 9cm cutter to stamp out rounds. If it's easier, divide the dough into four pieces and roll out the pieces one at a time.

Take half the pastry rounds and spoon the cheese filling on to one half of each round. Then take the rest of the pastry rounds and spoon the olive filling on to those. Close up the pastries, crimp the edges and brush them with beaten egg. Sprinkle with either nigella or sesame seeds. Transfer to a baking sheet and bake for 15 minutes until golden. Brush them again with the egg wash half way through, if you think they need it.

MAKES 36-40

 **TONY'S TIP**

You don't need any special equipment – if you don't have a cutter, you can use a glass to cut out the dough rounds. Any combination of ingredients you fancy can go inside them – spiced lamb, cheese and herb, or spinach and herb. Just remember not to overfill them so the filling remains intact. I also love to dip my samboussek in tahina or harissa.

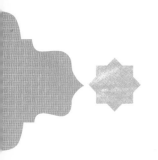

In the Middle East, falafel are eaten from dawn until dusk. They really are the poor man's bounty. I've made these extra special by filling them with cubes of salty feta and rolling them in nigella seeds.

Many people think that you make falafel from cooked chickpeas, but in fact we use dried chickpeas soaked overnight in lots of water. The pulses are mixed with flavourings to make them irresistible, then deep-fried. I serve them as part of a mezze, but they're equally delicious stuffed into pitta bread with a drizzle of natural yoghurt and some crisp salad vegetables. Serve with a tahina sauce to dip into or with salad and pitta.

# FETA & NIGELLA SEED FALAFEL

500g dried chickpeas
50g mild green chillies, halved, deseeded and roughly chopped
50g coriander, roughly chopped
50g onion (about ¼ of a large one), roughly chopped
25g garlic cloves (about 6)
½ tsp cumin
½ tsp coriander
1 tsp salt, plus extra to serve
175–250ml water
1½ tsp sesame seeds
¼ tsp nigella seeds, plus extra for rolling
150g feta, chopped into 1.5–2cm squares
vegetable oil, for frying

About 12 hours before you want to make the falafel, put the chickpeas in a bowl and cover with 750ml water. Soak for 12 hours.

Drain the chickpeas and put into a food processor. Add the chilli, coriander, onion and garlic, and whizz all the ingredients together until everything is finely chopped and the mixture looks slightly powdery. If it still looks like chopped nuts, whizz for a little longer.

Add the spices and salt, and with the motor running, gradually add the water until the mixture starts to stick together. You'll need to stop every now and then to check the stickiness of the mixture. Stir in the sesame and nigella seeds.

Take half the mixture and roll it on a board to make a long sausage about 3cm thick. Cut it into eight pieces, each weighing about 75g. Take one piece, flatten it slightly in the palm of one hand and push a cube of feta into the middle. Bring the flattened mixture around the feta to cover it. Sprinkle some nigella seeds on a plate and roll each ball lightly in the seeds. Set the balls aside on a plate, then continue making balls with the remaining pieces and feta. Repeat with the other half of the falafel mixture, rolling it out and shaping it into balls around the remaining feta cubes.

Heat the oil in a large saucepan or a deep-fat fryer until the temperature is 170°C, or test with a cube of bread that should turn golden in about 20 seconds. Fry the falafel in batches of four or five balls for 8–10 minutes until golden, then drain on kitchen paper. Sprinkle with salt before serving.

**SERVES 6**

When you're making a big spread of dishes for a mezze, it's good to have some that are simple to make but still full of flavour. This one ticks these boxes. It's made by coating slices of halloumi in the spice blend za'atar (made from thyme, sesame seeds, sumac and salt), then baking them until golden. They are delicious! Plus, if you fancy garnishing them with a little extra something, dot each piece with rose-petal jam.

# ZA'ATAR-CRUSTED HALLOUMI
## HALLOUMI BIL ZA'ATAR

250g block of halloumi
olive oil, for brushing
4–5 tbsp za'atar
a little rose-petal jam,
  to serve

Preheat the oven to 220°C/200°C fan/gas mark 7.

Cut the halloumi into 12 slices. This can be tricky, so I cut the block through the middle first, then cut each half into six slices.

Brush each slice with olive oil. Scatter the za'atar over a plate and press the slices in it until they're all covered. Spread them out on a lightly oiled baking sheet and bake for 8 minutes. Serve with a little rose-petal jam on each slice.

**SERVES 6**

I was brought up eating couscous, so it's hard to believe that when I first came to London no one had heard of it. Almost 30 years later I reckon it's cooked as often as pasta in most family homes.

For me, this recipe is best when I've taken the time to marinate the chicken the day before cooking. Not only does this infuse it with the flavours of the marinade, but it also ensures that it becomes extra tender on cooking. Tossed with roasted vegetables, couscous and fresh herbs, this makes a healthy and wholesome lunch or supper, and the best thing about it is that it can be scaled up if I'm cooking for a lot of people. If that's the case, I'll spoon the nuggets of chicken on top at the end and scatter over a few extra leaves of the herbs, plus a handful of pomegranate seeds – I love the way they glisten like jewels on top. I also find this a really useful recipe when I'm training for a marathon; I'll swap the couscous for quinoa for that extra nutritional boost.

# ROASTED CHICKEN & COUSCOUS SALAD SALATETE COUSCOUS BIL DAJAJ

FOR THE CHICKEN
juice of 1 lemon
2 garlic cloves, crushed
1 tbsp olive oil
1 tsp tomato purée
1 tsp each salt and black pepper
2 large chicken breasts, cut into 3cm cubes

FOR THE VEGETABLES & COUSCOUS
½ small butternut squash, chopped into 3cm cubes
2–3 tbsp olive oil, plus extra to drizzle over the salad and couscous
3 red onions, chopped into 3cm cubes
1 red and 1 green pepper, deseeded and chopped into 3cm cubes
200g couscous

Preheat the oven to 200°C/180°C fan/gas mark 6.

Put the lemon juice, garlic, oil, tomato purée, salt and pepper into a large bowl. Mash the tomato purée into the other ingredients using the back of a spoon, then add the chicken cubes and set aside to marinate. You can prepare this up to a day before, if you like.

Toss the squash with about ½ tablespoon of the oil in a bowl, then tip it into a roasting tin and roast for 10 minutes. Meanwhile, add the remaining vegetables to the bowl with the rest of the oil, season and toss well.

When the squash has been roasting for 10 minutes, add the other vegetables and any oil in the bowl to the tin and roast for a further 20 minutes until they're all tender and golden at the edges.

After the first 5 minutes, tip the chicken into a separate ovenproof dish and roast it underneath the vegetables for about 15 minutes until the pieces are golden and cooked through.

While everything's roasting, prepare the couscous. Put it into a large bowl, pour over the stock, cover with a lid and leave it to soak - it'll be ready to fluff up in about 15 minutes.

200ml hot chicken or
  vegetable stock
juice of 2 limes
4 spring onions, finely
  chopped
small handful of mint
  and coriander leaves,
  freshly chopped
1 tsp salt and a good
  pinch of black pepper

When the roasting time's up check the chicken - cut through a piece to make sure there are no pink juices remaining.

Use a fork to fluff up the couscous and separate all the grains. Pour over the lime juice and tip the spring onions into the bowl along with the herbs, some seasoning and a glug of olive oil. Spoon in the roasted vegetables and chicken. Carefully mix everything together, then spoon on to a large platter and let everyone help themselves.

**SERVES 4–6**

As a child, we always had
some sort of salad on the
table and the flavours
would change with the
seasons. The Middle
Eastern way of eating is
always very generous and
therefore these salad and
vegetable recipes provide
the perfect balance to
any meal – some are so
delicious you'll just want
to eat them on their own!

# SALADS & VEGETABLES

This recipe is a halfway house between a chopped salad and a dip. It's a bit unusual in that the only ingredient that's cooked is the aubergine. In the restaurants, we lay it on the charcoal grill and keep turning it until it's cooked all the way through, which infuses it with a wonderfully rich, smoky flavour, but at home you can do this under a very hot grill or on a barbecue. The important part is that the skin becomes blackened and blistered so that the flesh inside is completely cooked and the bitter-tasting juices that come out of the aubergines are drained away, otherwise the salad will be soggy.

# GRILLED CHOPPED AUBERGINE SALAD SALATETE EL RAHEB

vegetable oil, for rubbing
3 large aubergines
½ red and ½ green pepper, deseeded and finely chopped
4 spring onions, finely chopped
2 tomatoes, halved, deseeded and finely chopped
2 garlic cloves, crushed
small handful of chopped flat-leaf parsley
2–3 tablespoons extra-virgin olive oil
juice of ½ lemon
2 tbsp pomegranate molasses
1 tsp salt
handful of pomegranate seeds, to serve

Heat the grill until it's hot. Rub a little oil all over each aubergine, then place them on a baking sheet and grill until blackened and blistered. Cool a little, then peel away and discard the skins. Put the flesh in a colander over a bowl to drain away the juices.

Place the aubergine flesh on a board and chop finely. Put in a large bowl and add the chopped peppers, spring onions, tomatoes, garlic and parsley. Stir everything together to ensure that all the ingredients are evenly dispersed.

Add the olive oil, lemon juice, pomegranate molasses and salt, and stir everything again. Spoon into a bowl and garnish with the pomegranate seeds.

**SERVES 4–6**

My mum used to make a quick fried aubergine salad for me and my brothers when we dashed home for lunch on a school break. Later, leftovers would be stuffed into a sandwich, which of course were just as good. You probably know by now that aubergine is a star in my kitchen – fried, roasted or blackened and blistered until soft – I love it any which way. Here, I really take care over assembling the dish at the end. When I'm layering all the ingredients, I make sure that each slice of aubergine has a little of each one, so every mouthful is filled with all the flavours.

# AUBERGINE & POMEGRANATE SALAD
## SALATETE BATENJAN BIL ROMANE

2 tbsp olive oil, plus extra for frying
2 aubergines, sliced into 1cm rounds
½–1 red chilli, halved, deseeded and finely chopped
3 garlic cloves, chopped
25g shelled pistachio nuts, slivered
handful of pomegranate seeds
small handful of fresh mint leaves
2 tsp each lemon juice and pomegranate molasses
salt and black pepper

Heat 1 tablespoon of oil in a large frying pan. Season the aubergine slices and fry them in batches for 3–4 minutes on each side, until golden and tender, adding more oil as necessary. Take care when laying the slices in the hot pan as the hot oil can spit madly. Transfer them to a plate as each one is cooked.

Arrange the slices on a large platter, with each piece slightly overlapping another. Scatter over the chilli and garlic, followed by the pistachio nuts, pomegranate seeds and mint leaves.

In a separate bowl, whisk together the remaining oil, the lemon juice and pomegranate molasses and season. Drizzle over the salad and serve.

SERVES 4–6

If you ask anyone who comes from Libya, Morocco, Tunisia or Algeria, they'll each give you a different way of making this salad. And, in fact, when I was developing the recipe it went through various guises until I had it just the way I wanted.

I love the way crunchy, refreshing raw peppers can be transformed by grilling them until they're just charred and golden. The skins are then whipped off and the soft flesh combined with black olives, the delicate flavour of fresh mint and the scattered sliced chillies that give it that essential kick of heat.

# ROASTED PEPPER SALAD
## SALATETE MESHWIYA

2 large red peppers, halved, deseeded and quartered
2 large green peppers, halved, deseeded and quartered
75–100ml olive oil, plus extra to drizzle
1 large tomato, halved
1 red chilli, thinly sliced
1 green chilli, thinly sliced
handful of black olives, sliced
small handful of small mint leaves
extra-virgin olive oil, to drizzle
salt and black pepper

Preheat the oven to 200°C/180°C fan/gas mark 6.

Spread the pepper halves over a large baking sheet and drizzle with a little oil. Season well.

Roast in the oven for about 45 minutes until the skins have started to blister and char. After about 25 minutes, add the tomato halves, season, and continue to roast until the tomato is soft.

Put the peppers and tomato into a bowl, allow to cool a little, then remove and discard the skins. Chop the pepper and tomato flesh, put them in a bowl and stir in the oil.

Spoon into a serving bowl, top with the chillies, olives and mint leaves, and drizzle a little extra-virgin olive oil over the top.

**SERVES 6**

**TONY'S TIP**

I like this hotter and if you do, too, you can roast 1 or 2 extra chillies at the same time as the tomato. Just keep an eye on them so they don't burn or they'll be bitter.

**SALADS & VEGETABLES**

If you keep a couple of jars of ready-cooked beans in your kitchen cupboard, there's always the possibility of a feast. This salad is so simple, fresh, healthy and easy to make. All you do is add a rainbow of vegetables and a touch of garlic to the beans to create this substantial lunch. Great as part of a mezze or served with grills and roasts.

# BUTTER BEAN SALAD
## SALATETE FASSOULIEH BEYDA

2 x 400–500g jars
  butter beans, drained
  well
4 spring onions, finely
  chopped
1 red pepper, halved,
  deseeded and finely
  chopped
1 green pepper, halved,
  deseeded and finely
  chopped
3 tomatoes, halved,
  deseeded and finely
  chopped
small handful of parsley,
  finely chopped
2 tbsp olive oil
2–3 tbsp lemon juice,
  plus a couple of lemon
  wedges to serve
2 garlic cloves, crushed
1 tsp salt

Spoon the butter beans into a large serving bowl. Add the chopped spring onions, the peppers, tomatoes and parsley, and gently fold everything together.

In a separate bowl, whisk the olive oil, lemon juice, garlic and salt together, then pour over the salad and toss everything again gently.

Serve straight away at room temperature with the lemon wedges to squeeze over.

**SERVES 4–6**

**TONY'S TIP**
I love all kinds of beans and sometimes replace the butter beans with chickpeas or ready-cooked lentils.

If the sun is shining and there's a barbecue on the cards, then I have to make this. It's great with lamb, fish or any chicken dish and is just like a potato salad. Instead of mayo, we whisk tahina with water to make a sauce, then flavour it first with garlic – of course – and lots of parsley to turn it green. Then at the last minute we stir in lemon juice. The lemon thickens the sauce immediately, so don't add it any earlier. This recipe makes double the quantity you need for the spuds but it will keep well in a sealed container in the fridge for up to a week. It really is just like mayo, and totally addictive, so feel free to use it in exactly the same way.

# NEW POTATOES & GREEN TAHINA SALAD SALATETE BATATA BIL TAHINA KHADRA

500g small new
  potatoes, skins on
1 tbsp olive oil
1 garlic clove, crushed
salt and black pepper

FOR THE SAUCE
75g tahina
75–100ml cold water
1 garlic clove
½–1 tsp salt
large handful of chopped
  flat-leaf parsley,
  plus a little extra for
  sprinkling
juice of 1 lemon

TO SERVE
pinch of chilli flakes,
  to sprinkle
sumac, to sprinkle
extra-virgin olive oil,
  to drizzle

Bring a medium saucepan of water to the boil. Add the new potatoes, cover the pan and bring back to the boil. Once boiling, half cover the pan, turn down the heat to medium and simmer for about 15 minutes until the potatoes are tender. Drain, then return to the pan with the oil and garlic, and season well. Toss everything together and cover to keep warm.

Put the tahina into a bowl and add the water. Whisk together until it's smooth and the two ingredients become a creamy sauce.

Smash the garlic clove with the salt and whisk into the sauce. Add the chopped parsley and use a hand blender to blend everything together. Alternatively, transfer to a food processor to blend it – the sauce should be very green.

Put the potatoes in a dish, then add the lemon juice to the tahina sauce, spoon it over the potatoes and sprinkle a few small parsley leaves on top. Scatter over the chilli flakes and sumac, garnish with a few dots of extra-virgin olive oil and serve straight away.

SERVES 4–6

This is a very popular summer salad in the villages of Syria and the Lebanon, where villagers pick tomatoes from their own garden, still warm, and ripened by the sun until juicy and sweet. This might be the simplest salad you will ever make, but it's also one of the most delicious. Once you've made it, leave it on the side for 20 minutes or so to allow the juices of the tomatoes to run into the dressing for extra flavour.

# VILLAGE TOMATO SALAD
## SALATETE BANADOURA

red, green and yellow heritage tomatoes: 3 beef tomatoes, 4 vine tomatoes and 2 long vines of red and yellow medium cherry or midi plum tomatoes
3 garlic cloves
1½ tbsp sumac, plus extra to sprinkle
75ml extra-virgin olive oil
1 tsp cider vinegar
squeeze of lemon juice
½–1 long mild green chilli, thinly sliced
2 spring onions, sliced
small handful of young mint sprigs, leaves picked
salt and black pepper

Slice the tomatoes and arrange them on a plate so you have a really good balance of colour between the red, yellow and green tomatoes.

Crush the garlic with a bit of salt and some freshly ground black pepper. Put in a bowl and stir in the sumac, then add the olive oil, cider vinegar and a squeeze of lemon juice, and whisk together.

Drizzle the dressing over the tomatoes, then scatter the chilli over the top, followed by the spring onions and the mint leaves. Finally, be generous and sprinkle extra sumac on top of the tomatoes before serving.

SERVES 6

Halloumi is to the Lebanese what mozzarella is to Italians. I love the way the taste of halloumi turns from soft and salty to sweet and caramel-like when it's pan-fried until golden. To give it that savoury edge, I marinate the slices first in thyme and seasoning before they go in the pan. While they're cooking I take sprigs of cherry tomatoes and cook them just until the skins burst and blister, then arrange them on top of the slices. It's a very simple dish, loaded with flavours and textures, and I always make it when I have friends over at home.

# GRILLED HALLOUMI WITH ROASTED VINE TOMATOES
## HALLOUMI MESHWY BIL BANADOURA

8–10 sprigs of thyme
2 tsp olive oil, plus a
   little extra for frying
2 x 250g blocks of
   halloumi
2–3 vines of cherry
   tomatoes
salt and black pepper

Pull all the leaves off the thyme and put in a large, shallow bowl. Add the oil and season with salt and pepper.

Slice each pack of halloumi into eight or nine pieces and lay the slices in the oil mixture, rubbing it all over each piece. This can be done up to a day ahead.

Heat a frying pan until hot and fry the halloumi pieces for 1–2 minutes on each side until golden. Arrange on a plate.

Meanwhile, heat a drop of oil in another frying pan and fry the cherry tomato vines until the tomatoes are cooked and the skins have blistered. Season, then lift them out and arrange on top of the halloumi, and serve straight away.

SERVES 6

 **TONY'S TIP**

I also like to serve halloumi with roasted peppers, so if you fancy those, here's how to prepare them. Preheat the grill to very hot. Cut 1 or 2 red peppers into quarters and remove the seeds. Rub a little oil over each piece and season with salt and black pepper. Transfer to a baking sheet and grill until the skin has blistered and the peppers have softened. Peel off the skin when cool enough, if you like. Serve the peppers alongside the halloumi.

SALADS & VEGETABLES

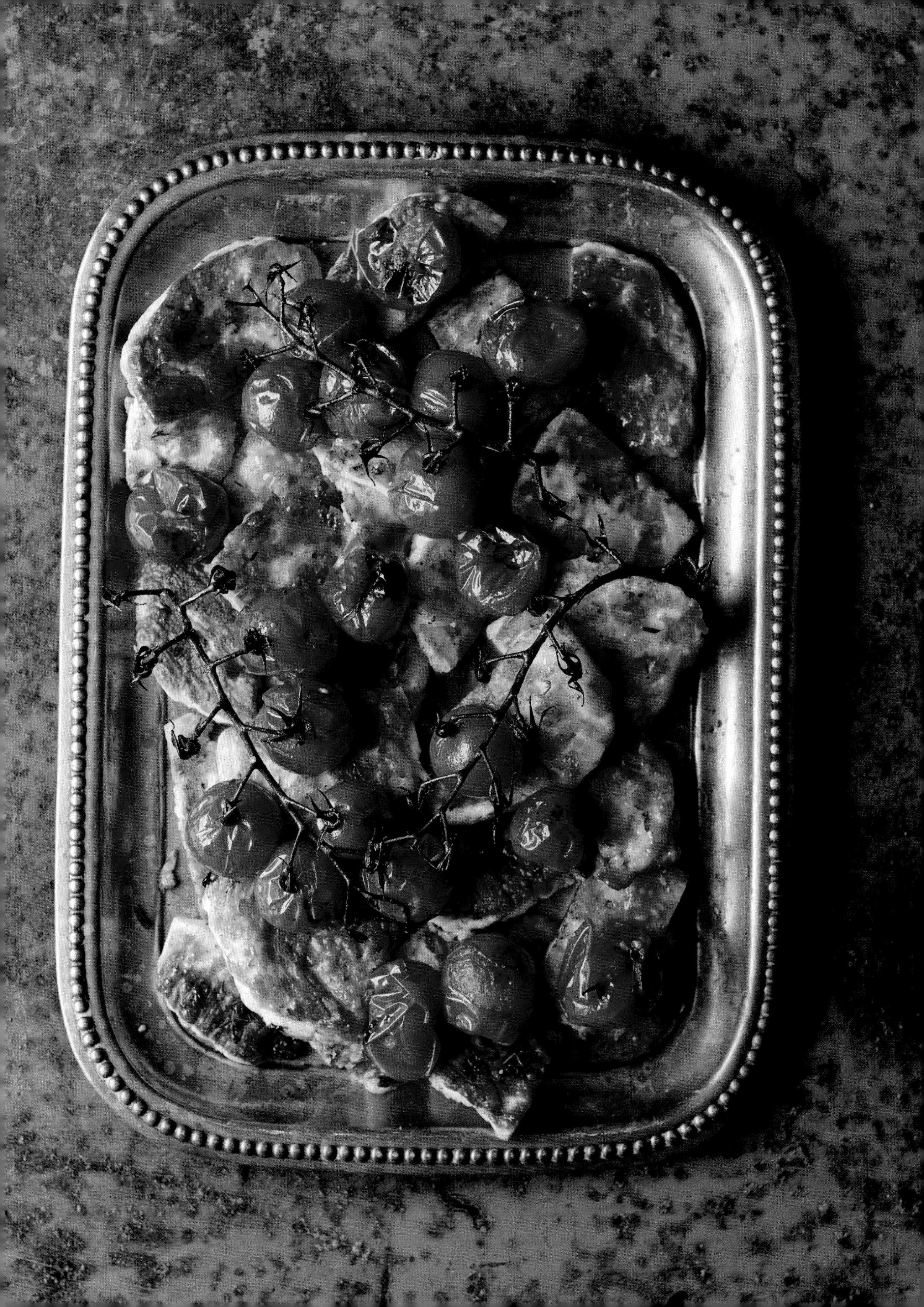

This salad features one of my favourite fruits, figs, which I remember picking as a child. We would fill buckets with the most delicious, just soft, green and black fruits plucked straight from the trees. Back home, my mum would set to work and make fresh-tasting jams, sometimes with the addition of walnuts, and sometimes with a dash of rose water. In late summer and early autumn when figs are in season, I always make this.

Dark rounds of sliced beetroot form the base, then it's topped with pops of colour in the form of sweet cherry tomatoes, caramelised figs, small green mint leaves and a highlight of crumbled feta. It's important to scatter each ingredient evenly over the top when you're putting this together, so that everyone gets a good selection of the different flavours. If you can't find figs use roasted apricots, peaches or pears.

# BEETROOT, FIG & FETA SALAD
## SALATETE SHOUMANDAR WA TEEN

a generous knob of
  butter
1 tsp caster sugar
2 just-ripe figs, each cut
  into 6–8 wedges
500g cooked beetroot,
  thinly sliced
125g red and yellow
  cherry tomatoes,
  halved
100g feta, crumbled
2 tbsp toasted sesame
  seeds
3 tbsp olive oil
2 tbsp cider vinegar
1 tsp runny honey
paprika, to season
small handful of small
  mint leaves, to serve

Melt the butter in a frying pan and sprinkle over the sugar. As soon as the butter has stopped foaming, carefully lay the fig wedges in the butter and cook for 1–2 minutes on each side until just golden.

Take the slices of beetroot and arrange them on a large platter, with each slice slightly overlapping the next. I find it easier to start by laying the slices on the outer edge of the platter and then work in so that they're all lying on top of one another.

Place the cherry tomatoes over the beetroot slices, then scatter over the feta. You can do this with your hands or use a spoon, if you prefer. Sprinkle the sesame seeds over the top.

Whisk the olive oil, vinegar and honey together and spoon over the top, then season with paprika. I like to sprinkle this on the feta so the white of the cheese is highlighted by the red spice. Finally, arrange the mint leaves on top and serve.

**SERVES 6**

This typical Lebanese dish is, in my opinion, the best way of using up a home-grown glut of green beans or runner beans at the height of summer. Mum used to cook it a lot and sometimes studded it with chunks of slow-cooked lamb. The sauce is made with fresh sun-ripened tomatoes and lots of garlic, softened first with onion in plenty of olive oil. This dish is best served warm or cold, so that the taste of the olive oil really comes through, along with the flavours of the other ingredients.

# FRENCH BEANS IN A TOMATO & OLIVE OIL SAUCE LOUBIA BELZEYT

500g tomatoes
50ml olive oil
½ large onion, sliced
7 garlic cloves, sliced
1kg green or runner beans, trimmed and roughly chopped
175ml water
1 tbsp tomato purée
1 tsp salt
½ tsp black pepper

Start by preparing the tomatoes. Cut a cross in the top and bottom of each tomato and put them in a large bowl. Cover with boiling water and leave for 1½–2 minutes. Drain well and cool, then slip off and discard the skins. Chop the tomatoes and set aside.

Heat the olive oil in a large saucepan and sauté the onion and garlic over a low-to-medium heat for 4–5 minutes until starting to colour. Stir the beans into the onion mixture, along with the water, then cover with a lid and continue to cook over a low heat for 5–8 minutes. It's important to let the beans cook through at this stage; once you add the tomatoes they'll take much longer.

When the beans are very tender, add the chopped fresh tomatoes, the tomato purée and seasoning. Stir well and cook for a further 10 minutes to allow the tomatoes to cook down and all the flavours to meld together.

SERVES 6

 TONY'S TIP

Sometimes I like to finish this dish by topping it with grilled plum tomatoes. Make sure your grill is really hot, then cut a couple of ripe plum tomatoes through the stalk. Drizzle with a little oil and season well, then grill until golden and soft. Spoon the stewed beans into a large serving bowl, top with the tomatoes and scatter over some coriander.

I've always loved broad beans the way my mum used to cook them when I was a child – steamed, then mixed with couscous. This recipe is a bit unusual in that it uses the pods that encase the broad beans. They give a beautiful texture to the whole dish and, being packed with garlic, olive oil and lemon juice, it is really healthy. I like a lot of lemon juice, so I always pour in the juice of two lemons at the end. But if you prefer a more subtle taste, pour in the juice of just one lemon and taste to check it's how you like it. You can eat it on its own, or serve it with couscous, generous glugs of olive oil over the top and a glass of laban (drinking yoghurt) on the side.

# BRAISED BROAD BEANS WITH OLIVE OIL FOOL AKDAR BIL ZEYT

2kg young broad beans
  in their pods
4 tbsp olive oil
1 large onion, chopped
10 garlic cloves, chopped
2 tsp salt
1 tsp white pepper
150ml water
small bunch of coriander,
  chopped
juice of 1–2 lemons

Take half the broad beans, pod them and set them aside – there's no need to slip each bean out of its skin. Take the other half and cut the top and bottom off each pod, discard the ends, then pull the string down on each side and discard that, too. Chop the pods into 4-5 pieces.

Heat the olive oil in a large saucepan and sauté the onion and garlic for 5 minutes over a medium heat. Add all the prepared broad beans, the salt and white pepper, and sauté over a low heat for 3-4 minutes. Cover the pan and leave to cook over a low heat for 5 more minutes.

Add the water, cover again, and leave to cook for a further 40 minutes. Check whether everything is cooked. The stew should not be completely dry, so add more water and simmer until heated through, if need be.

Finally, stir in the coriander and as much of the lemon juice as you like. Serve warm or cold.

SERVES 6–8

I've never forgotten my grandad walking into the kitchen with his arms wrapped round huge bundles of green vegetables from the farmers' market. Grandma would make light work of chopping them and cooking them until tender, and then dress them in a very simple way with just olive oil, seasoning and a touch of garlic.

You need big, firm full-flavoured greens for this recipe – the ones that are a bit tough when raw, but hold their shape when blanched and sautéed. I often use Swiss chard, but if I go to a specialist greengrocer and can get my hands on collard greens or green leafy endive, I'll plump for those. This really is one of my favourite dishes and, to be honest, I love it so much I could eat a whole bowlful in one sitting.

# BRAISED GREENS IN OLIVE OIL
## HINDBE BELZEYT

1kg Swiss chard, collard
    greens or green leafy
    endive
2 tbsp olive oil
1 medium onion, sliced
2 garlic cloves, crushed
a lemon wedge
½ tbsp salt
pinch black pepper

TO SERVE
sunflower oil, for deep-
    frying
1 onion, thinly sliced
a lemon wedge

Bring a large saucepan of water to the boil. Half-fill a large bowl with ice, then top it up with cold water to make an ice bath.

Trim the tough stalks from the greens and discard them, then chop the remaining leaves. Blanch them in the boiling water for 1 minute. Drain and spoon them straight into the ice bath. Drain well.

Heat the olive oil in a large saucepan and sauté the onion and garlic over a low heat for 10–15 minutes.

Squeeze the water out of the greens, then stir them into the pan with the onions and garlic. Squeeze over the juice from the lemon wedge, add the salt and pepper, and stir everything together. Cover the pan with a lid and simmer over a low heat for 10 minutes. Taste to check the seasoning.

Pour enough oil into a medium saucepan to come about 5cm up the side. Heat the oil until the temperature reaches 190°C or a piece of bread browns in 10–15 seconds. Carefully, lower half the onion slices into the oil and cook until golden. Spread out on kitchen paper to drain while you cook the rest of the slices.

Spoon the hindbé into a bowl, top with the fried onions and serve with an extra lemon wedge.

**SERVES 6**

This salad is really healthy and I'll even eat it for breakfast sometimes. It can be knocked up in minutes and features some of my favourite summer ingredients – crisp radishes and sharp spring onions, together with sweet, blushed-from-the-sun tomatoes. In place of spicy black pepper, musky, aromatic cumin is whisked together with lemon, olive oil and garlic, which perfectly seasons the dressing.

# FUL SALAD WITH RADISH
# & MINT SALATETE FUL

juice of 1 lemon
2–3 tbsp olive oil
1 garlic clove, chopped
½ tsp salt
a pinch of cumin
400g tin ful (broad
  beans), drained
200g chickpeas, drained
8 cherry tomatoes,
  chopped
2 spring onions, chopped
4 radishes, thinly sliced
1 sprig of mint

Put the lemon juice, olive oil, garlic, salt and cumin in a large bowl. Whisk everything together and taste to check the seasoning.

Add the beans, chickpeas, tomatoes, spring onions and radishes.

Toss everything together gently to mix all the ingredients well.

Pull the leaves from the mint and chop roughly. Scatter over the salad, toss again and serve. If you have time, set the salad aside for 5 minutes so that the ingredients marinate in the dressing and mint leaves.

**SERVES 6**

I love my peppers roasted until they're so soft that they melt in the mouth. The smell and taste of extra-virgin olive oil reminds me of holidays, and the pomegranate molasses adds a touch of sweetness, as well as being one of my very favourite flavourings.

# ROASTED PEPPER & FETA SALAD
## SALATETE FELAFELA MESHWY

8 large red peppers, halved, cored and deseeded
olive oil, for grilling
200g feta cheese
small bunch of flat-leaf parsley, chopped
3–4 tbsp extra-virgin olive oil
1–2 tbsp pomegranate molasses
paprika, to sprinkle
salt and black pepper

Heat the grill until very hot. Cut the pepper halves in two so you have smaller pieces – they're much easier to roast when they're this size.

Rub the skins with a little olive oil, then put on a baking sheet skin-side up and grill until the skins are dark and blistered. Slide them into a bowl, cover with a lid and leave for about 30 minutes for the skins to steam off. Remove and discard the skins.

Arrange the skinned peppers on a plate, scatter over the feta, then the parsley. Season with salt and black pepper, and drizzle with extra-virgin olive oil and pomegranate molasses. Finally, sprinkle with paprika to serve.

**SERVES 6**

**SALADS & VEGETABLES**

Okra is very like Marmite, isn't it? Some of my friends love it and some hate it. And I have to admit I never liked the texture when I was little. I love it now, though, and this is a very handy mezze dish to know how to cook, especially if you keep a bag of frozen baby okra in your freezer. I find that the smaller okra have a less slimy texture than the larger ones, plus if you stir-fry them first until golden, they stay tender. They're still delicate, though, so when you're making this, try not to stir the okra too hard or they'll start to break up.

# BRAISED OKRA WITH TOMATO SAUCE BAMIA BIL ZEYT

1kg tomatoes
3 tbsp olive oil
1kg baby okra, thawed if frozen
1 onion, chopped
10 garlic cloves, chopped
2 tbsp tomato purée
1 tsp salt
½ tsp black pepper
100ml water
handful of coriander, chopped, plus extra to garnish
extra-virgin olive oil, to drizzle

Start by skinning the tomatoes. Cut a cross in the top and bottom of each one, then put them into a large bowl. Pour over enough boiling water to just cover, then leave for about 1½–2 minutes.

Drain the tomatoes and rinse in cold water. Carefully peel off and discard the skins. Chop the tomatoes.

Heat 1 tablespoon of olive oil in a large frying pan and fry the okra in two batches until just golden, tossing every now and then. Tip into a bowl as you cook each batch.

Pour the remaining oil into a large saucepan and heat gently. Stir in the onion and garlic, and sauté over a medium heat for 8–10 minutes until starting to turn golden. Add the chopped tomatoes, tomato purée, salt and black pepper, and return the okra to the pan. Pour in the water.

Stir all the ingredients together, cover with a lid, then bring to a simmer and cook for 10 minutes. Stir in the coriander and cook over a low heat for a minute or two more and it's done. Garnish with extra coriander and a drizzle of extra-virgin olive oil.

SERVES 4–6

Some of my favourite recipes, such as this one, are those that have been passed on through families. This came via our Syrian chef, Wassim – it's his mother's dish – and he often makes it for me in the restaurant. Instead of chopping the aubergines into chunks or slicing them into rounds, he cuts them lengthways into wedges, which gives the whole salad a meatier look. You can either deep-fry the wedges or roast them, as I've suggested here, then drizzle them with a simple onion, tomato, garlic and chilli dressing. Add tender grilled lamb chops or skewers of grilled, marinated chicken on the side for the perfect feast.

# SYRIAN AUBERGINE SALAD
## SALATETE BATENJAN

3 large aubergines
3 tbsp olive oil
¼ onion, finely chopped
1 garlic clove, finely chopped
1 green chilli, halved, deseeded and finely chopped
150g tomatoes on the vine, finely chopped
1 tbsp cider vinegar
½ tsp salt
1–2 tbsp extra-virgin olive oil
small handful of flat-leaf parsley, chopped

Preheat the oven to 200°C/180°C fan/gas mark 6.

Cut each aubergine in half lengthways, then slice each half into three wedges lengthways. You'll have 18 long, thin wedges by the time you've finished.

Arrange the aubergine wedges in a large roasting tin and drizzle over the oil. Season well and roast for 45 minutes–1 hour, until the aubergines are really soft.

While the aubergines are roasting put the onion, garlic, green chilli and tomatoes into a bowl. Stir in the vinegar and ½ teaspoon salt.

When the aubergines are ready, arrange them on a warmed plate. Stir the extra-virgin olive oil and chopped parsley into the dressing, then spoon over the aubergine. Serve straight away.

**SERVES 6**

Lots of my friends are so-so about cauliflower ... until I serve them this. What makes it unique is the tahina dressing. Here, the humble cauli is carved into wedges, deep-fried until golden, then smothered in a smooth tahina sauce. It's essential to season the wedges as soon as they're cooked so they soak up any additional oil from frying. I love the way the cauliflower becomes tender but wonderfully flavoursome and sweet when fried, which is a great match for the nutty, savoury taste of the sauce.

# CAULIFLOWER & TAHINA
## ARNABIT BIL TARATOR

vegetable or sunflower
  oil, for deep-frying
1 large cauliflower

FOR THE TARATOR SAUCE
40g tahina
50–60ml cold water
¼ tsp salt, plus extra to
  sprinkle
small handful of chopped
  flat-leaf parsley
juice of ¼ lemon
2 spring onions, thinly
  sliced
1 red chilli, halved,
  deseeded and thinly
  sliced

Pour enough oil into a saucepan or deep-fat fryer to cook the cauliflower and heat to about 180°C or until a cube of bread browns in about 10 seconds.

Remove and discard the cauliflower leaves and cut it in half through the middle, then cut each piece in half again so you have four pieces. Fry the cauliflower pieces all together, if they will fit in the pan, otherwise fry them in batches. Drain on kitchen paper and sprinkle with a little salt.

Whisk the tahina and water in a bowl. Stir in the salt and parsley, followed by the lemon juice.

Position the cauliflower on a plate so that it looks whole again. Spoon over the sauce, sprinkle with the spring onions and chilli, and serve.

SERVES 4–6

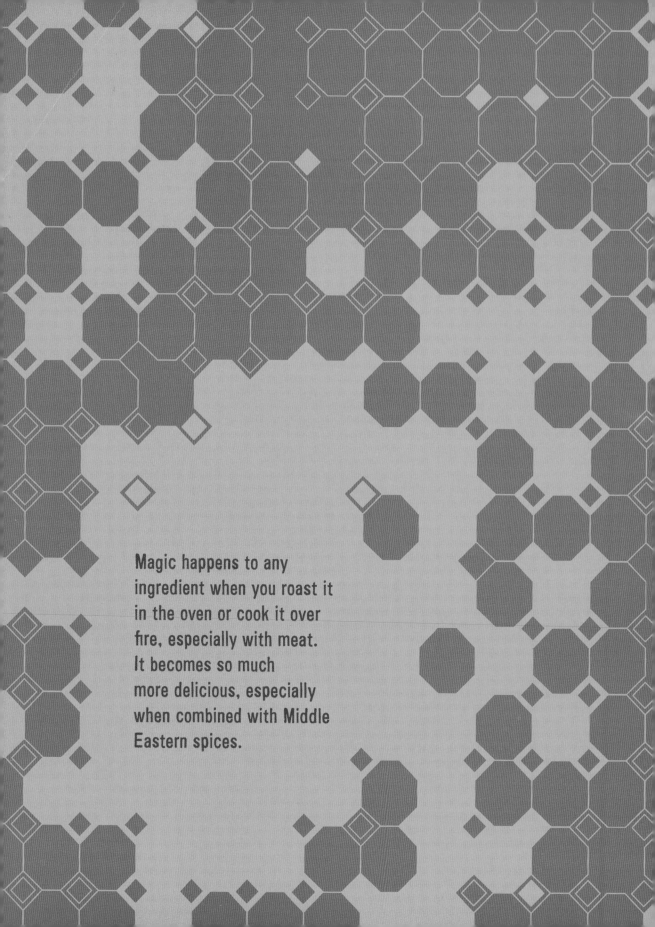

Magic happens to any ingredient when you roast it in the oven or cook it over fire, especially with meat. It becomes so much more delicious, especially when combined with Middle Eastern spices.

# ROASTS & GRILLS

We've been serving this in our restaurant for more than 18 years now and it's so good, so popular, that I don't think we'll ever take it off the menu. In our culture we don't serve our meat pink or medium; it's always well done. So in this recipe the joint is cooked until crispy on the outside, moist on the inside and soft enough to be shredded with a fork.

This recipe really sums up what this book is all about – layers of flavour in one huge feast of a dish, brought to the table accompanied by a wonderful array of sides to complement it (see photo on pages 122–3).

# SLOW-COOKED SHOULDER OF LAMB KATAF GHANAM MESHWY

### FOR THE MARINADE
½ onion, roughly chopped
3 garlic cloves
½ bunch of coriander, roughly chopped
20g root ginger, chopped
¼ tsp cumin
½ tsp ras-el-hanout
¼ tsp cinnamon
¼ tsp turmeric
¼ tsp Lebanese seven-spice mix
1 tsp salt
¼ tsp white pepper
½ tsp black pepper
50ml vegetable oil
2–2.5kg shoulder of lamb, bone in

### FOR THE SAUCE
25ml vegetable oil
25g butter
½ red onion, chopped
1 carrot, chopped
2 garlic cloves, chopped
4–5 sprigs of thyme

Up to two days before you serve the lamb, marinate the shoulder. Put the onion, garlic, coriander, root ginger, spices, salt, peppers and oil into a mini blender and whizz to make a paste. Put the shoulder into a large sealable container and rub the paste all over it. Cover and chill for at least 24 hours and up to 48 hours.

Take the lamb out of the fridge so that it comes up to room temperature – if it's too cold, it will take longer to cook. When you're ready to cook it, preheat the oven to 220°C/200°C fan/gas mark 7.

Put the lamb in a roasting tin and roast in the oven for 20 minutes until it has coloured on all sides.

While the lamb is cooking in this short blast of heat, make the sauce. Heat the oil and butter in a medium saucepan and sauté the onion, carrot and garlic for 10 minutes over a medium heat until starting to soften and turn golden. Stir in the thyme sprigs, tomato purée and the tin of tomatoes, then fill the tin with hot water twice (making about 800ml of water in total) and pour that into the pan, too. Stir in the coriander and parsley, and bring to the boil. Simmer, half covered with a lid, for 15 minutes. Blend until smooth using a hand blender.

When the lamb has cooked for 20 minutes, take it out of the oven and pour the sauce over it. Cover the tin tightly with foil, reduce the temperature to 170°C/150°C fan/gas mark 3 and return the lamb to the oven. Cook for about 3 hours until very tender. After each hour, remove the tin to check the meat and pour in 500ml boiling water,

2 tbsp tomato purée
400g tin chopped
   tomatoes
small handful of
   coriander, chopped
small handful of flat-leaf
   parsley, chopped

FOR THE DRIED FRUIT
4 each dried apricots,
   dried figs, dates and
   prunes
handful of golden raisins
1 cinnamon stick
2 whole star anise
1 tsp rose water
2 tbsp honey

FOR THE RICE
1 tbsp vegetable oil
½ onion, finely chopped
150g lamb mince
1 tsp salt
½ tsp black pepper
good pinch of Lebanese
   seven-spice mix
1 tsp ras-el-hanout
200g basmati rice
25g toasted mixed nuts
handful of fresh mint
   leaves

TO SERVE
Greek yoghurt
harissa
toasted sesame seeds

stirring it into the sauce. Turn the shoulder over, and spoon the sauce all over it. You'll know it's ready when you can push your finger through the side of the shoulder easily because the lamb has become very tender.

The next step is to prepare the fruit to go on top of this dish. Put all the dried fruit into a small saucepan, add the cinnamon, star anise, rose water and honey and enough cold water to just cover the fruit. Cover the pan with a lid and bring to a simmer. Simmer for 10–15 minutes to allow the fruit to plump up. Set aside to cool.

About 45 minutes before the lamb will be ready, cook the rice. Heat the oil in a medium saucepan and sauté the onion for 5–8 minutes. Add the lamb mince, breaking it down with a spoon so it browns evenly, then stir in the spices and seasoning. Cook for about 1 minute, then stir in the rice. Once the rice is coated with oil and mixed into the spiced onion and lamb mixture, cover with 500ml boiling water. Put a lid on the pan, bring the liquid to the boil, then turn the heat down low and simmer for 10–12 minutes. Turn off the heat under the pan and set aside.

When the lamb is ready, take the roasting tin out of the oven and strain off the sauce. Keep it warm.

Take a large platter and spoon the rice all the way round the edge. Lift the lamb into the middle. Arrange the dried fruit around it, then scatter the nuts and mint over the top. Serve with the warm sauce, yoghurt, harissa and a sprinkling of toasted sesame seeds.

**SERVES 6**

### TONY'S TIP

The lamb will be at its best if you marinate it first for at least a day, and is even better if you marinate it for two days. As there's quite a bit of work involved in putting this together, I also suggest that you make the sauce (which is poured over the lamb during roasting) at the same time, then seal it in a container and chill it. You can cook the dried fruit in advance, too, and set it aside at room temperature in a covered container.

This recipe is perfect for so many occasions, whether it's a casual Saturday or Sunday lunch, or when you're having a larger number of people over. Any leftovers can be sliced and stuffed into a flatbread with salad and a drizzle of tahina the next day. I've taken seasoning to another level here by chopping up lots of garlic, chilli and peppers, cooking them lightly in olive oil, then rubbing them all over the whole chicken before roasting it in the oven. Serve the roast chicken on a bed of sliced tomatoes scattered with chopped coriander. You'll need four or five medium or large tomatoes on the vine. You might have too much sauce, but it keeps in the fridge.

# SPICED ROAST CHICKEN
## DAJAJ MASHWI

6 tbsp olive oil, plus a
little extra for greasing
2 red and 2 green
peppers, halved,
deseeded and finely
chopped
2 mild long green and
2 red chillies, halved,
deseeded and finely
chopped
8 garlic cloves, chopped
small handful of
coriander, finely
chopped, plus extra to
garnish
1 whole chicken,
about 1.5kg, at room
temperature
1 tsp salt
½ tsp black pepper

Preheat the oven to 200°C/180°C fan/gas mark 6.

Start by making the sauce. Heat the oil in a frying pan and sauté the peppers, chillies and garlic for 10–15 minutes until softened. Stir in the coriander and season. Spoon into a bowl and set aside to cool.

Put the chicken into a roasting tin, then rub a little oil over the skin and season with the salt and pepper.

Spoon about three-quarters of the sauce over the top and generously massage the mixture into the chicken, both inside and outside. The more you rub it in, the better the flavour will be. You can do this 2–3 hours ahead of cooking, if you want. Pour a large glass of water into the tin, too. This will help to stop the juices burning. Cover with foil and roast for 1 hour. Remove the tin from the oven, take off the foil and return the chicken to the oven for about 30 minutes.

Remove the tin from the oven and check that the chicken is cooked by piercing the thigh to see whether the juices run clear. If they're still pink, return the chicken to the oven and continue to check every 5–10 minutes until it's done. The chicken should have a really good colour and be golden on the outside.

Lift the chicken on to a plate, cover with the foil again and rest for 10 minutes, then carve into slices and serve.

**SERVES 6**

This very unusual dish, made with a generous amount of lemon juice, was cooked by our Syrian chef, Wassim, whose mother used to cook it for him and the family when he was little. It's great if you're cooking for a crowd as it's so easy to multiply the quantities.

Pieces of baby chicken, marinated first to tenderise them, are roasted in the oven on top of rounds of thickly sliced potato. The spicing is subtle – small quantities of spices to season the meat – and the most important ingredients are the lemon juice, olive oil and garlic. The unique balance of the ingredients is key to the success of this dish.

# BABY CHICKEN WITH LEMON JUICE & POTATOES
## SAYNIA DAJAJ WA BATATA

6 garlic cloves
1 tsp salt
½ tsp Lebanese seven-spice mix
½ tsp allspice
½ tsp black pepper
juice of 4 large, ripe lemons
150ml olive oil
2 small chickens, 1.2kg each, jointed
1.5kg potatoes, peeled and cut into 1.5cm-thick slices
1 lemon, cut into 6–8 thin slices
small handful of fresh mint or flat-leaf parsley, to serve

Crush the garlic cloves with the salt, then put into a large sealable container. Add the spices and black pepper, then stir in the lemon juice and 75ml of the olive oil. Mix everything together well.

Add the jointed baby chicken, cover and leave to marinate for at least 1 hour. If the chicken has been stored in the fridge, it'll be fine in a cool kitchen for an hour. If you're going to cook it later, put the container in the fridge to chill, then take it out of the fridge about half an hour before you plan to cook the chicken.

Preheat the oven to 200°C/180°C fan/gas mark 6.

Heat half the remaining oil in a pan and fry the potato slices in batches for 2 minutes on each side, adding more oil as needed and placing them in an ovenproof dish or roasting tin once they're done.

Arrange the chicken pieces on top of the potatoes, with a slice of lemon tucked between each one. Pour the marinade over the top. Roast in the oven for 20 minutes, then turn the chicken over and roast again for a further 15–20 minutes until the chicken is deep golden and cooked through.

Scatter over the mint and serve.

SERVES 6

I first tried this dish at the home of my Palestinian friend Haleem many years ago. His mum cooked it for me, and I was so blown away by the flavours that I now make it whenever I have a lot of people over. Once you've tried it, you will always remember the taste because it's so unusual. It is a typical Palestinian dish, but it's also popular in other countries in the Middle East. Traditionally this is made with village bread, but you can also make this with Arabic bread, as I did here.

# PALESTINIAN BRAISED SPICED CHICKEN PIE MOUSSAKHAN

1kg boneless, skinless chicken, chopped into large chunks
150ml olive oil
juice of 2 lemons
2 garlic cloves, crushed
2 tsp salt
½ tsp black pepper
1.5kg onions, sliced
70g sumac
1 tbsp cinnamon
¼ tsp cardamom
50ml pomegranate molasses
50g pine nuts, plus extra to garnish
1 packet of village bread or Arabic bread
½ tsp black pepper
chopped flat-leaf parsley, to garnish

Preheat the oven to 200°C/180°C fan/gas mark 6.

Put the chicken in a bowl and add 50ml of the olive oil, the lemon juice, garlic, 1 teaspoon salt and the black pepper, and mix together.

Transfer to a roasting tin and spread it out over the base. Cook in the oven for 20 minutes until the chicken is tender. Use two forks to pull apart the largest piece to check it's cooked through the middle.

Meanwhile, heat the remaining 100ml of olive oil in a medium frying pan and fry the onions over a gentle-to-medium heat until they're very soft. This will take a good 20 minutes; make sure they don't burn or turn too golden. Keep stirring them every now and then. They should be so soft that when you put them in your mouth, they melt.

Take the chicken out of the oven and shred it with two forks or use a knife to cut it into pieces.

If there's a lot of juice in the pan, drain it off. Stir in the sumac, cinnamon, cardamom, pomegranate molasses, pine nuts and onions, and mix really well to ensure that the sumac coats all the ingredients.

Unwrap the village bread – it's very thin and delicate so be careful you don't tear it – and lay two layers of bread in a round 20–22cm cake tin. Spoon the chicken filling into the middle and spread it into the corners with the back of a spoon. Fold the edges over the chicken, then top with another layer of bread. Cover the tin with foil and bake in the oven for 15–20 minutes. Take the foil off for the last couple of minutes to allow the top to crisp up slightly before serving.

**SERVES 6-8**

These Syrian meatballs are simple to make but really delicious. I first tried it at my friend Talal's house in Damascus; his wife Alia is an amazing cook. She served it with spiced rice and lots of home-baked flatbread.

There are two parts to this recipe – prepping the mix for the meatballs then shaping them, and making the sauce. So if you want to split the work involved to get ahead, it's easy to do. You can marinate the lamb up to a day beforehand and shape the meatballs – just keep them stored in an airtight container in the fridge. Similarly, you can make the sauce, cool it quickly, and again store it, chilled, until you're ready to use it. Then, all you need to do is cook and serve. (See photo on pages 132–3.)

# SPICED MEATBALLS IN TOMATO SAUCE KABAB HINDI

FOR THE MEATBALLS
**500g lamb mince**
**½ onion, finely chopped**
**½ tsp salt**
**½ tsp cinnamon**
**½ tsp Lebanese seven-
   spice mix**
**½ tsp allspice**
**½ tsp black pepper**
**25g pine nuts, plus 25g
   extra to serve**
**oil, for drizzling**

Start by making the meatballs. Put all the ingredients into a bowl and mix everything together with your hands. Squeeze the mince to make sure that all the spices and seasoning are mixed well through the meat. Cover the bowl and set aside.

Next, make the sauce. Cut a cross in the top and bottom of each tomato and put in a large bowl. Cover with boiling water and leave to soak for 1½–2 minutes. Drain, then slip off and discard the skins. Chop the tomatoes and put in a bowl.

Melt the butter in a large saucepan and sauté the onions over a medium-high heat for 5 minutes until they are starting to turn golden. Stir in the garlic and cook for 1 minute, then add the peppers, chilli, salt and pepper and cook for a further 5 minutes, stirring every now and then to stop them sticking to the base of the pan.

At this point, preheat the oven to 240°C/220°C fan/gas mark 9 – this may seem high but the temperature needs to be nice and hot to cook the meatballs quickly.

Spoon the tomatoes and all the juices into the pan, give everything a good stir, then cover with a lid and cook over a low-to-medium heat for about 15 minutes, again stirring every now and then, until the tomatoes have cooked down and thickened into a sauce.

1kg tomatoes – plum or
  large tomatoes on the
  vine
50g butter
1½ onions, thinly sliced
5 garlic cloves, thinly
  sliced
1 green and 1 red pepper,
  halved, deseeded and
  thinly sliced
1 red chilli, halved,
  deseeded and thinly
  sliced
1½ tsp salt
½ tsp black pepper

While the sauce is cooking, shape the meatballs. Take a piece of the mince mixture, a little bigger than a walnut and a little smaller than an apricot, and put it into the curve of your hand where the fingers meet the palm. Squeeze it into the shape of a rough oval. Put it on a plate and do the same with the rest of the mixture. You should be able to make about 24 meatballs from this quantity.

Drizzle a little oil into a roasting tin and brush over the base. Put the meatballs in the tin and bake in the oven for 5 minutes, until they just start to colour. Scoop out on to a plate, then spoon the tomato sauce into the tin. Put the meatballs back on top, spaced evenly apart, then cover with foil and return to the oven for 15 minutes. Remove the foil, then return to the oven again for 2–3 minutes more. Serve scattered with the extra pine nuts.

**SERVES 6**

## TONY'S TIP

If you're going to serve this with rice, you can cook it while the lamb and sauce are in the oven. Pour 300g basmati rice into a medium pan, then add 600ml boiling water and ½ teaspoon of salt. Cover with a lid, bring to the boil, then turn down the heat to low and cook for 10–12 minutes until all the liquid has been absorbed. Fluff up with a fork to serve.

I've eaten these in lots of places, including Istanbul and Syria, but it was in a small village outside Beirut that the kebabs were the most memorable. My friend Abdu and his wife, Samar, invited me over, and Samar told me that they'd picked the aubergines for the dish in the morning. Not only that, the meat had also come from a butcher who slaughtered a lamb every morning before delivering it to the house. Cooked on a charcoal grill, it was the freshest kebab I've ever eaten. I particularly loved the way the charcoal infused the meat with a smoky flavour.

# AUBERGINE & SPICED MINCED-LAMB KEBABS KEBAB BATNJAN

**FOR THE KEBABS**
500g lamb mince
1 small onion, finely chopped or grated
bunch of flat-leaf parsley, finely chopped
1 tsp salt
1 tsp cinnamon
½ tsp Lebanese seven-spice mix
½ tsp allspice
½ tsp black or white pepper
olive or vegetable oil, for frying
1–2 Chinese aubergines, sliced into 3cm rounds

**FOR THE SALAD**
½ red onion, thinly sliced
½ red and ½ green pepper, deseeded and thinly sliced
2 tbsp cider vinegar
pepper paste or harissa, for spreading
1 tbsp extra-virgin olive oil
salt and black pepper

Start by marinating the salad. Put the onion, peppers and vinegar into a bowl and season with salt and pepper. Set aside.

Next, make the kebabs. Put the mince into a large bowl and add the onion, parsley, salt, cinnamon, seven-spice mix, allspice and pepper. Use your hands to mix everything together until the spices and onion have seasoned the meat well. Set aside.

Heat the grill until it is hot.

Meanwhile, heat a little oil in a frying pan over a medium heat and fry the slices of aubergine for 1–2 minutes until golden on both sides. Cool a little.

Divide the mince mixture into 18 pieces and roll each piece into a barrel about the same thickness as the slices of aubergine and about 5-6cm long. Thread them on to skewers, alternating with the aubergine slices. I usually manage to push 3 koftas and 2-3 aubergine slices on to each skewer.

Place the skewers on a baking sheet and grill until golden all over, turning after 10 minutes, then cooking again for 10 minutes on the other side. Set aside to rest.

Spread the paste thinly over the flatbreads. Drain the vinegar from the onion salad and stir in the oil. Spoon evenly over the flatbreads. Slide on to a separate baking sheet and grill for a few minutes until the breads start to crisp up just at the edges.

ROASTS & GRILLS

6 flatbreads or 2 village
  breads
parsley, to sprinkle
1–2 tbsp pomegranate
  molasses
handful of pomegranate
  seeds
50g toasted pine nuts
  (optional)

Place the flatbreads on a board, top with the skewers, then scatter over the parsley. Drizzle over a little pomegranate molasses and scatter over the pomegranate seeds and the pine nuts, if using.

**SERVES 4–6**

Fresh fish and seafood are a
delicious part of Middle Eastern
cookery that bring together
more delicate spicing and subtle
levels of flavour. It can often be
cooked so quickly – ideal for a
midweek supper – or used in more
indulgent weekend recipes.

# FISH
# &
# SEAFOOD

I first tasted this in a small seaside village in Lebanon. Sliced onions are slow-cooked until they're beautifully caramelised, then tahina is stirred in. I particularly love the combination of the soft flesh of the bream and the silky texture of the sauce. I use a lot of lemons, both for the marinade and the sauce. Remember when you're tasting the sauce that it needs to taste of tahina, but it must also retain the flavour of the lemon juice and garlic.

# BAKED BREAM WITH TAHINA SAUCE TAJEN SAMAK

2 garlic cloves, crushed
juice of 2 lemons
1 tsp cumin
2 tbsp olive oil
small bunch of coriander, chopped and divided in half
3 large sea bream, gutted and slashed twice on each side
25g pine nuts, toasted, to garnish

FOR THE SAUCE
100g tahina
2 garlic cloves, crushed
200–300ml water
juice of 2 lemons
70ml olive oil
1kg onions, thinly sliced
salt and black pepper

Start with the tahina sauce. Put the tahina in a bowl, add the garlic, water and lemon juice, and whisk together. Season well and set aside.

Next, marinate the fish. Put the garlic, lemon juice and cumin in a bowl. Stir in the olive oil then add half the coriander. Put the fish in a roasting tin, pour the marinade over and inside each fish and rub in. Set aside.

To finish the sauce, pour the olive oil into a frying pan, add the onions and cook over a steady, medium heat, stirring regularly until caramelised. This will take from 50 minutes to an hour. Don't rush. The onions will shrink to a quarter of their original volume, and become golden and really soft.

While the onions are cooking, preheat the oven to 200°C/180°C fan/ gas mark 6.

Roast the fish for about 20 minutes, until the flesh is opaque and tender.

When the onions are caramelised, add the tahina sauce to the pan. Cook over a low-to-medium heat, pushing a wooden spoon underneath so it doesn't stick. Any wateriness will disappear as you continue to cook until oil comes to the top when it starts to boil. This will take 10–15 minutes. Turn off the heat and stir in more of the coriander, keeping a little to scatter over the top.

Take the fish out of the oven and arrange it on a platter. Spoon the sauce over the top, scatter over the pine nuts and remaining coriander, and serve.

SERVES 6

This is the king of seafood dishes, and if you like the French fish soup bouillabaisse I guarantee you'll love this. There's no need to make a base fish stock from lots of shells for this one — just add the fish to the stew so that it simmers and infuses the stew with lots of flavour. I've used chopped squid and whole prawns in the sauce, along with chopped new potatoes. I like to cook the fish separately, so I can marinate it first in lemon juice, olive oil and garlic, then arrange it on top of the stew to serve. I love mine spicy with lots of harissa.

# SEAFOOD STEW YAKNATT SEMAR AL BAHAR

**FOR THE SAUCE**
5–6 tomatoes
50ml olive oil
1 onion, chopped
4 garlic cloves, chopped
2 small squid tubes, chopped
2 prawns in their shells
2 tsp cumin
1 tsp salt
½ tsp white pepper
1 tsp tomato purée
8–10 new potatoes, halved or quartered, depending on size
handful of coriander, roughly chopped
about ¼ pomegranate

**FOR THE FISH**
25ml olive oil
juice of 1 lemon
1 garlic clove, crushed
1 tsp salt
3 salmon fillets
3 sea bass fillets
6 large king prawns

Start by marinating the fish. Put them in a large, shallow bowl. Mix the olive oil, lemon juice, garlic and salt together, pour over the fish and set the bowl aside in a cool place.

Next prepare the tomatoes for the sauce. Make a cross in the top and bottom of each, then put them in a bowl and cover with boiling water. Leave to soak for 1½ –2 minutes, then drain away the water and peel the skins. Cut the tomatoes in half, scoop out and discard the seeds, then roughly chop the flesh. Set aside.

Heat the oil in a large sauté pan with a lid, add the onion, garlic, squid and prawns, and stir-fry for 10 minutes.

Stir in the cumin, salt, pepper and tomato purée, and mix everything together, then spoon in the chopped tomatoes and pour 350ml boiling water into the pan. Cover with a lid and bring to a simmer over a medium heat, then reduce the heat and cook for 1 hour.

After 30 minutes, add the potatoes to the pan, give everything a stir again, then continue to cook over a low heat with the lid off the pan.

About 20 minutes before the stew has finished cooking, heat the grill until it's hot. Put the salmon, sea bass and prawns on a baking sheet and grill until golden.

Spoon the sauce and potatoes into a large, warm serving bowl, then top with the fish. Scatter over the coriander, separate the seeds from the skin of the pomegranate and arrange over the top, then serve.

**SERVES 6**

Sultan Ibrahim is what the Lebanese call red mullet, and it's also their national fish dish. Every restaurant serves its own recipe. You order it by the kilo, rather than by the portion, and it will be brought to the table on a large platter with a bottle of arak, the Levantine aniseed-flavoured spirit.

# FRIED RED MULLET WITH CRISP BREAD & TAHINA SULTAN IBRAHIM

6–12 red mullet (about 2kg), cleaned and scaled
sunflower oil, for frying
3–4 tbsp plain flour, seasoned with 1 tsp salt and 1 tsp cumin
1 large village bread, cut into 6 pieces, or 6 flatbreads
1 lemon, halved

FOR THE TABBOULEH
2–3 large bunches of flat-leaf parsley
leaves of ½ bunch of mint
50g fine cracked wheat
4 large, ripe tomatoes, finely chopped
5–6 spring onions, finely chopped
juice of 1½–2 lemons
1½ tsp salt
100ml olive oil

FOR THE TAHINA SAUCE
100g Greek yoghurt
150g tahina
1 garlic clove, crushed
small handful of flat-leaf chopped parsley

Start by making the tabbouleh, as the cracked wheat needs time to soak in the dressing so that it swells until tender. Chop the parsley and mint very finely on a board. Don't overchop and go over the herbs a second time once you've chopped them, otherwise they will become soggy and won't provide the right texture for the tabbouleh.

Wash the herbs well, then spoon them into a sieve resting over a bowl. Sprinkle over the cracked wheat and leave on the worktop for 30 minutes to 1 hour to allow the wheat to absorb the moisture.

Meanwhile, make the tahina sauce. Stir the Greek yoghurt, tahina, garlic and parsley together, then add a good splash of water to loosen the mixture. Set this aside, too.

Check the fish for any stray scales and throw them away. Heat a couple of centimetres of oil in a large frying pan. It's ready when a piece of bread sizzles madly in it. Spread the flour mixture on a large plate. Dip each fish into it to coat both sides, then shallow-fry the fish on both sides to get the skin nice and crispy and cook the flesh all the way through.

Once all the fish has been fried, fry the pieces of bread until just golden. Season with a little salt.

Finish the tabbouleh. Tip the herbs and cracked wheat into a large bowl. Add the tomatoes, spring onions, lemon juice, salt and olive oil, and mix everything together.

Spoon the tabbouleh on to a large platter, carefully arrange the fish on top followed by the crisp bread and serve with the tahina sauce and lemon halves to squeeze over.

**SERVES 6**

This dish has held special memories for me since I was a little boy. We lived in a flat in Tizi Ouzou and we'd know when the sardine seller was coming from his shout, 'Yalla, yalla, yalla'. Everyone would gather where he set down his stall, and some mums would drop a basket on a rope from the high windows of homes with money in exchange for the fresh fish. A little while later when I walked into the building, I'd smell the wonderful aroma of sardines frying wafting down the central staircase. Every home would cook them in exactly the same way, but the flavours would vary depending on the different spices they used.

# MY MUM ZOHRA'S FRIED SARDINES

24 garlic cloves
1 tbsp paprika
a pinch–¼ tsp crushed
  chillies, depending on
  how much heat you like
2 tbsp salt, plus extra
  for sprinkling
2–3 tbsp olive oil
75ml water
about 1kg small sardines
  (8–12cm long),
  cleaned and gutted,
  with head and tail on
1 tbsp cumin
300g plain flour, plus
  extra for rolling
vegetable oil, for frying
1 lemon, halved

TO SERVE
chopped flat-leaf parsley
harissa

Put the garlic cloves into a large mortar and crush with the pestle to make a paste. Add the paprika, chillies and 1 tablespoon of salt, and mix together with the olive oil and water.

Put the paste into a sealable container, add the fish, then toss everything together. Do this a good 1–2 hours before you plan to cook them, to allow the fish to marinate in the paste.

Mix the cumin, flour and remaining tablespoon of salt in a large bowl. Pick out the larger sardines, dip them in the flour and lay them on a separate tray. Do this until you've coated about 600g of the sardines in flour.

Take the remaining 400g sardines, open them out, remove the head and bones and chop the flesh. Add them to the bowl of flour then start to knead the mixture, as you would if you were making bread dough. The idea here is to completely break down the sardines to make a smooth, doughy mixture that you can roll out to make galettes.

Lightly flour a board. Split the dough into three and roll out each piece out until it's really thin – about 3–4mm. Use a 10cm cutter to make six rounds, re-rolling the dough as necessary.

You cook this recipe in two parts – first the sardines and then the galettes. Heat some oil in a deep-fat fryer until it's about 170°C or until a cube of bread sizzles madly when you drop it in. Pick up the sardines by their tails and drop them gently one by one into the oil, and cook until golden – about 3–5 minutes.

Heat 1½–2 cm oil in a large frying pan over a medium heat and fry the galettes for 4–5 minutes on both sides until golden. Test by slicing one in half and having a taste – they should be crispy and cooked all the way through.

Sprinkle both with a little salt once they're cooked.

Dip the lemon halves into a little chopped parsley. Scatter the rest of the parsley over the sardines and serve with the galettes, lemon halves and a bowl of harissa, if you like more spice.

**SERVES 6**

I love the texture of cuttlefish – it's just like squid – and the flavours of the lemon, garlic and coriander in this dish are so light. This is a perfect summer recipe, particularly because it's so quick and easy to make. Cuttlefish needs to needs to be cooked either quickly over a high heat, as in this recipe, or braised long and slow so that it's really tender. If the cuttlefish is already prepared and cleaned, this short, sweet and very delicious recipe can be on the table and ready to eat in about 15 minutes. Now that's what I call fast food!

# CUTTLEFISH WITH GARLIC, LEMON & CORIANDER HABAR BIL TOUM WA LEYMOON

100ml olive oil
1kg cuttlefish, cleaned
  and cut into even-sized
  5cm pieces
½ tbsp salt
1 tsp black pepper
2 garlic cloves, crushed
juice of 2 lemons, plus
  lemon wedges to serve
¼ bunch of coriander,
  chopped
1 mild red chilli, sliced,
  to serve

Heat half the oil in a large frying pan over a medium-to-high heat. Fry the cuttlefish very quickly until golden on both sides.

Season with the salt and pepper, then stir in the garlic and cook for 1 minute. Stir in the remaining oil, the lemon juice and most of the coriander, then cover the pan with a lid and simmer for 5–7 minutes … and that's it!

Spoon into bowls, scatter over the chilli and the remaining coriander, and serve with the lemon wedges.

**SERVES 6**

Once you've tried it, I promise that you'll love making this dish again and again for friends and family. You need to ask the fishmonger to give you a bag of bones when you buy the fish so you can make stock.

# SEA BASS WITH SPICED RICE SAYADIEH

**FOR THE SEA BASS**
2 garlic cloves, crushed
juice of 1 lemon
1 tsp cumin
small bunch of coriander, chopped
25ml olive oil
½ tsp salt
good pinch of black pepper
6 large sea bass fillets – ask the fishmonger for the bones
small handful of chopped flat-leaf parsley and pomegranate seeds, to serve

**FOR THE RICE**
25ml olive oil
2 onions, finely chopped
500g basmati rice
1 tsp salt
1 tsp cumin
juice of 1 lemon

**FOR THE STOCK & SAUCE**
50ml olive oil
2 onions, sliced
1 garlic clove, chopped
500g fish bones
1½–2 litres boiling water
1 lemon, chopped
1 tsp cumin
1 tsp cornflour

Start by making the stock. Heat the oil in a large saucepan and sauté the onions until they turn a dark golden colour. Scoop out a spoonful (about a third) to use as garnish later.

Stir in the garlic and cook for 1 minute. Add the fish bones, the boiling water, the lemon and the cumin, and cover the pan with a lid. Bring to the boil and simmer, half-covered, for 1 hour.

Next, marinate the sea bass. Put the garlic, lemon juice, cumin, coriander, oil, salt and pepper into a shallow container. Stir everything together. Add the fillets and toss to coat. Cover and chill until you're ready to cook them.

When the stock is cooked, strain it into a bowl. Now it's time to cook the rice. Heat the olive oil in a saucepan and sauté the finely chopped onions until golden. Stir in the rice, the salt and cumin and cook for 1 minute. Pour 1 litre of stock into the pan and stir everything together.

Cover with a lid and bring to a simmer. Turn the heat down very low and cook for 12 minutes. Turn off the heat, squeeze over the juice of a lemon and leave the rice to steam.

While the rice is cooking, heat the grill until it's very hot. Take the fish fillets out of the marinade, lay them on a baking sheet and grill until the flesh is opaque, 5–10 minutes.

Pour the rest of the stock into a clean saucepan and place over a low heat. Put the cornflour into a small bowl and stir in a couple of tablespoons of the cold stock. Stir this to make a thick sauce, then pour it back into the stock to thicken it slightly.

When you're ready to serve, spoon the rice into bowls, top with the fish, then spoon over the sauce and finish with a few of the reserved onions and a sprinkling of parsley and pomegranate seeds.

**SERVES 6**

When I was growing up, prawns were a luxury. I don't think I had them more than six times at home in the first 18 years of my life in Algeria. My parents couldn't afford to buy them regularly, so it was only when they had friends and family over for a special occasion that we'd enjoy them. But I have fond memories of fennel. At my grandparents' house we would eat it in stews, in salads and even raw as a snack. This dish is a marriage of these two gorgeous ingredients. It's a very simple and delicious fish stew, with a wonderful garlicky tomato base.

# SAUTÉED PRAWNS WITH SPICED BRAISED FENNEL

2 tbsp olive oil, plus
  extra for brushing
1 large onion, chopped
6 garlic cloves, chopped
6 very ripe, large
  tomatoes
1 litre hot fish stock
2 tbsp tomato purée
2 tsp salt
1 tsp black pepper
1 tsp cumin
1kg whole, raw king
  prawns
2 large bulbs fennel,
  cut into wedges, core
  removed
bunch of coriander,
  chopped

Heat the oil in a large saucepan and sauté the onion and garlic over a low-to-medium heat for 5–8 minutes until starting to turn golden.

Meanwhile, prepare the tomatoes. Cut a cross in the top and bottom of each one and put them in a large bowl. Pour enough boiling water over the top to cover, then leave for 1½–2 minutes, then drain well. Carefully peel away and discard the skins, then chop the flesh.

Add the chopped tomatoes to the pan, stir everything together and cook for a further 3–4 minutes until the tomatoes have started to cook down.

Pour in the fish stock, then add the tomato purée, salt, pepper and cumin. Stir everything again, then cover to bring the liquid to the boil quickly. Take the lid off the pan and reduce the heat so the stew is simmering, then cook over a low heat for 15–20 minutes to allow the flavours of the stock to deepen.

Meanwhile, heat a griddle pan until hot. Brush the prawns and fennel with oil. Griddle the fennel wedges on both sides in batches, setting each batch aside on a plate as it's cooked. Add the fennel to the stew and cook for a further 15 minutes or until tender. While the fennel is simmering in the stew, griddle the prawns in the same way.

Stir the coriander into the stew, then carefully place the prawns in, too, and cook for a further 5 minutes. You may need to turn over any prawns on the top, if they are just peeking out of the stew, so they cook evenly. Taste to check the seasoning, then serve.

**SERVES 6**

This recipe is very easy to do. The monkfish is marinated in my favourite spices for extra flavour. I like to serve it on a bed of braised fennel, onions and peppers, cooked until the fennel is so soft that it melts in your mouth.

# MONKFISH & ROASTED PEPPER KEBAB KIBAB SAMAK

2 bulbs fennel, cut into
  wedges, core removed
2 medium onions, each
  cut into wedges
600g vine tomatoes, cut
  into wedges
2 red peppers, seeded
  and cut into wedges
120ml extra-virgin olive
  oil
1 tsp salt
½ tsp black pepper
4 garlic cloves, sliced
leaves from 4 sprigs of
  thyme
12 Kalamata olives
small handful of
  coriander, to serve

FOR THE MONKFISH
2 tbsp olive oil
juice of 1 lemon
2 tsp coriander
2 garlic cloves, crushed
1 tsp salt
about 1.2 kg trimmed,
  boneless monkfish tail
3 marinated red peppers,
  halved and each half
  cut into 6

SERVES 6

Preheat the oven to 200°C/180°C fan /gas mark 6.

Put the fennel, onion, tomatoes and peppers into a large roasting tin. The vegetables should sit quite snugly together, rather than being spaced apart as for roasting. Pour over the oil, then season with the salt and pepper. Stir everything together and roast for 30 minutes.

Meanwhile, marinate the fish. Stir the olive oil, lemon juice, coriander, garlic and salt together in a large, sealable container. Cut the monkfish into pieces, each about 3cm square. You may find this easier if you first cut the piece of monkfish into six chunks, then divide each chunk up into squares to end up with the right amount for six skewers. Put the fish into the container and chill to marinate while the vegetables are in the oven.

When the vegetables have roasted for 30 minutes, remove the tin from the oven and stir in the garlic, thyme leaves and olives. Return to the oven and cook for a further 30 minutes.

About 15 minutes before the vegetables will be ready, preheat the grill.

Push a piece of monkfish on to a skewer followed by a piece of pepper and repeat until you have a total of six pieces of each on the skewer. Do the same with the rest of the monkfish and peppers until you've filled all the skewers.

Grill the skewers until the fish is opaque – about 5 minutes, turning them halfway through.

Divide the braised vegetables and skewers among six bowls then scatter the coriander over the top to serve.

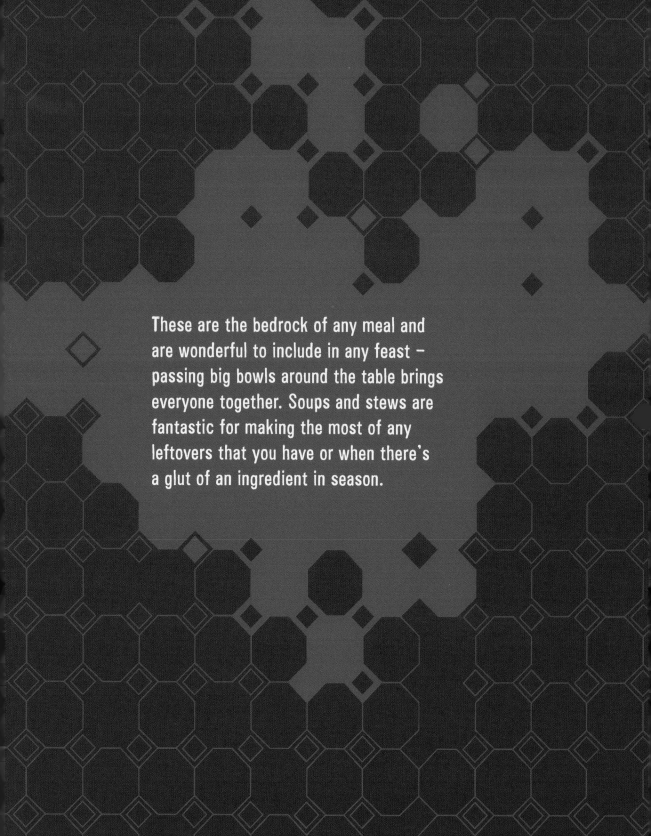

These are the bedrock of any meal and
are wonderful to include in any feast –
passing big bowls around the table brings
everyone together. Soups and stews are
fantastic for making the most of any
leftovers that you have or when there's
a glut of an ingredient in season.

# SOUPS
# &
# STEWS

This is particularly popular in Lebanon, and it's very healthy. It doubles as a main meal, if you add chicken or lamb. It's so easy to make, and you'll find variations on the ingredients depending on where you go. The main one, dried lentils, can be either red or green – it really doesn't matter – and it's a bonus that they don't need to be soaked first, so this can be rustled up in about half an hour. (See photo on page 156.)

# LENTIL SOUP WITH LEMON
## SHORBAT ADAS BIL HAMOOD

100ml olive oil
1 onion, chopped
250g green or red lentils
1½–2 litres hot water
1 medium potato,
  chopped
1 bunch of Swiss chard
  (about 100g), chopped
1½ tsp salt
½ tsp black pepper
6 garlic cloves, crushed
large handful of
  coriander, roughly
  chopped
juice of 1 lemon

Heat half the olive oil in a medium saucepan and sauté the onion for about 5 minutes until starting to soften. Stir in the lentils and ensure that they are coated in the onion oil, then cook for 1 minute.

Pour in the hot water, cover the pan with a lid and bring to the boil. Turn down the heat and simmer for about 10 minutes until the lentils are partly cooked. Add the potato, chard and seasoning, cover again, and continue to simmer for 10–15 minutes until the lentils are completely cooked.

Heat the remaining oil in a frying pan and stir in the garlic. Fry until just golden – it won't take long, so watch it carefully – then add the coriander. Stir this mixture immediately into the soup and simmer for 2–3 minutes. Pour in the lemon juice and simmer for a further minute. Serve straight away or, if you prefer, blitz until smooth.

**SERVES 4–6**

If you're going to make soup, you may as well make a big batch of it. That's what my mum always did to ensure that if we asked for seconds there was plenty to go round. This is so filling and warming that in our house we ate it as a main course. When I came to make it myself, I added tahina. The richness, in terms of both flavour and texture, provides an unusual dimension. I've always enjoyed this soup made with the hearts of fresh artichokes, but definitely feel it's all the better with a swirl of tahina to liven it up. (See photo on page 156.)

# ARTICHOKE & TAHINA SOUP
## SHORBAT KHARSHOOF BIL TAHINA

10 globe artichokes
50g butter or 50ml oil
1 onion, chopped
4 garlic cloves, chopped
2 celery sticks, chopped
½ leek, chopped
1 tsp salt
½ tsp black pepper
1 litre hot chicken or
  vegetable stock

FOR THE TAHINA SAUCE
75g tahina
100ml water
½ garlic clove, crushed
¼ tsp salt
juice of 1 lemon

TO SERVE
pinch of sumac
olive oil, for drizzling
juice of 1 lemon
  (optional)

Pull all the leaves from the artichokes and scrape out the furry chokes; discard these, if you're not using them for stock. Peel the outside of the artichoke hearts to remove the tough skin and chop them roughly.

Heat the butter or oil in a medium saucepan and sauté the onion, garlic, celery and leek over a medium heat for about 10 minutes, until the onion starts to soften. Turn the heat down to low if the onion starts to burn at any stage.

Season with salt and pepper, and pour in the stock. Bring to a simmer and cook, covered, for 10–15 minutes, or until the artichokes are tender.

Meanwhile, make the tahina sauce. Spoon the tahina into a bowl and stir in the water a little at a time until you have a smooth sauce. You might not need all the water. Add the garlic, salt and lemon juice, stir again and taste to adjust the seasoning, adding a little more tahina if it needs it, too. (Store any leftovers in a sealed container in the fridge, for up to a week.)

Use a stick blender to whizz until smooth. Stir in the tahina sauce and sumac, drizzle over a little oil, then taste to check the seasoning and stir in enough lemon juice to balance all the flavours, if you like. Serve with a swirl of tahina.

SERVES 6–8

Squashes and pumpkin give soup a really great thick texture, which is what I particularly love about this one. The base – onion, garlic, celery and leek – features in many of my soup recipes. I love the way the flavours soften and sweeten when cooked over a low heat and, once whizzed with the main ingredient, provide body and texture (see photo on page 157). Although I've suggested using either vegetable stock (if you're serving this to vegetarians) or chicken stock, sometimes I just use water. As long as the seasoning is right the soup will still be delicious.

# PUMPKIN & SAFFRON SOUP
## SHORBAT LAKTEEN WA ZAAFRANE

50ml vegetable oil or
  50g butter
1 onion, chopped
4 garlic cloves, chopped
2 celery sticks, chopped
½ leek, chopped
1kg baby squash or
  pumpkin, peeled
1 litre hot vegetable or
  chicken stock, or water
2 tsp salt
1 tsp black pepper
good pinch of saffron,
  plus a little extra to
  garnish

Heat the oil or butter in a medium saucepan over a medium heat and sauté the onion, garlic, celery and leek for about 5 minutes until starting to soften. If you're using butter, you may need to turn the heat down low so the butter doesn't burn.

Stir in the chopped squash or pumpkin, making sure it's coated in the vegetable mixture, and cook for a minute or so. Pour in the hot stock, season, add the saffron and cover with a lid. Bring to the boil then turn the heat down low and simmer, half covered, for 15 minutes until the squash is tender.

Cool the soup a little, then blend until smooth. Ladle into bowls and serve with a little extra saffron on top.

**SERVES 6-8**

I particularly love this soup because it can be served in two ways. On a hot day in summer, I serve it chilled straight from the fridge with crudités, such as carrot, cucumber and celery sticks, halved radishes and sometimes crispy pitta bread. When autumn comes, the weather cools but tomatoes are still around, it's delicious warm, too. It's pretty healthy and I've even been known to enjoy it at breakfast time. Take care not to cook the mint for too long – it should be added right at the end, just before blitzing the soup – otherwise it will taste bitter. (See photo on page 163.)

# TOMATO & MINT SOUP
## SHORBAT BANADORA WA NAÂNÂA

1kg tomatoes
25ml vegetable oil or
   25g butter
½ onion, chopped
2 garlic cloves, chopped
1 celery stick, chopped
¼ leek, chopped
1 tbsp tomato purée
1 tsp salt
½ tsp black pepper
600ml hot vegetable or
   chicken stock
leaves from 3 sprigs
   of mint, plus extra to
   garnish
4 tbsp olive oil

TO SERVE
a little feta, crumbled
pinch of paprika

Start by preparing the tomatoes. Cut a cross in the top and bottom of each tomato and put them in a large bowl. Cover with boiling water and leave for 1½–2 minutes. Drain well and cool, then slip off the skins and discard them. Chop the tomatoes and set aside.

Heat the oil in a large saucepan and cook the onion, garlic, celery and leek for about 5 minutes until starting to soften. Stir in the chopped tomatoes, the tomato purée and seasoning, and cook for a further minute or two.

Pour in the stock, stir, and cover the pan with a lid. Bring to a simmer, then cook over a low heat for about 15 minutes.

Cool the soup a little, then blend until smooth. Put the mint leaves in a blender with the olive oil and blend to make a mint dressing. Stir about three quarters of this into the soup to give it a fresh mint kick.

Ladle the soup into bowls and serve with a few mint leaves, some crumbled feta – it's so light it should float on top – and a pinch of paprika sprinkled over the top. Serve the remaining dressing alongside.

SERVES 6

Soothing and nourishing, you'll often find this soup being made by grandmas and mamas in Lebanon. It's very simple, but the flavour relies heavily on the quality of the stock, so I either make my own or use a very good fresh stock. It's a handy recipe to have in your collection as you can make just one large chicken breast and a handful of vermicelli pasta stretch to serve six people. Taste before adding the lemon juice, then squeeze in as much or as little as you need.

# LEBANESE CHICKEN SOUP
## SHORBAT DAJAJ

50ml oil or 50g butter
200g chicken breast, diced
1 onion, finely chopped
2 celery sticks, finely chopped
4 garlic cloves, crushed
1 tsp salt
½ tsp black pepper
100g vermicelli pasta
2 litres hot chicken stock
lemon juice, to season
small handful roughly chopped flat-leaf parsley, to serve

Put a splash of the oil into a frying pan and heat until hot. Add the chicken breast and cook until golden. Season with a little of the salt and pepper and set aside.

Put the remaining oil in a medium saucepan and add the onion, celery and garlic. Sauté over a medium heat for 8–10 minutes, until starting to soften.

Season with the remaining salt and pepper, then stir in the vermicelli and the stock. Cover with a lid and bring to a simmer. Cook for 3 minutes or so, or according to the instructions on the pasta packet.

Stir in the chicken and heat through, then season with the lemon juice, to taste. Finally, stir in the parsley and serve straight away.

SERVES 6

**TONY'S TIP**

You can buy two types of vermicelli – the nests and the small pieces. The small pieces are best for this, but if you can't get hold of them, break up a nest with your hands.

I'm addicted to making this stew with lamb in it now, but when I was growing up, meat was expensive, so my mum would make a vegetarian version. I love it even more this way. There's nothing fancy about this, which is why quite often I'll serve it in a big bowl plonked in the middle of the table and give everyone a spoon to dig in and share the wonderful flavours. Bread is, of course, essential to dip into the delicious juices, too.

# LAMB & ARTICHOKE STEW
## YAK NATT EL KHARSHOOF BIL LAHAM

3 large globe artichokes
juice of ¼ lemon
40g ghee or butter
100ml olive oil
6 lamb shanks, meat removed and cut into 3cm cubes, skin discarded
1 large onion, finely chopped
3 garlic cloves, chopped
2 tsp cinnamon
1 tsp salt
½ tsp black pepper
2 litres hot vegetable stock
1 litre water
3 medium carrots, chopped into 5cm chunks
300g fresh, podded peas
300g fresh, podded broad beans
½ bunch of flat-leaf parsley

Start by preparing the artichokes. Put them on a board and pull off the outer leaves one by one. You can discard these or use them to make a light stock. Once you've taken them all off, use a spoon to scoop out the hairy choke of each artichoke. Discard this, too, as it's not edible.

Peel and trim the stems, which otherwise will be woody and chewy. Put the artichoke hearts in a bowl of cold water and squeeze in the lemon juice to stop them oxidising and turning brown. Set aside.

Put a large saucepan over a medium heat, add the ghee and olive oil and, once the ghee has melted, brown the pieces of lamb until they are golden all over.

Add the onion to the pan and stir, then add the garlic, cinnamon and seasoning, and mix everything well. Allow the onion to cook over a medium heat for about 5 minutes. Pour the vegetable stock and the water into the pan, then cover with a lid and simmer gently for 1 hour. This is the important bit, as cooking the lamb over a low heat will make it very tender.

Lift the artichoke hearts out of the water and drain, cut them in half, then cut each half into three wedges. This will give you 18 wedges. Add to the pan, along with the carrots. Cover again and simmer for a further 30 minutes. Finally, add the peas and broad beans, and cook for a further 10-15 minutes, on a very low heat.

Turn off the heat, chop the parsley and sprinkle over the top, to serve.

**SERVES 6**

Our Middle Eastern equivalent of the burger, the kofta, comes in various shapes and sizes and flavoured with different spices, too. It's a key part of this recipe, which I think is a feast in the true sense of the word. Sliced potatoes, koftas and tomatoes are layered and cooked in a tomato sauce. This is perfect for a large family gathering, especially when you have kids. When I make it at home I have lots of harissa on the side, although my nephews always ask me for ketchup. Look out for the pepper paste to make this recipe in Turkish shops.

# SPICED LAMB KOFTAS WITH POTATOES & TOMATOES
## KOFTA BIL SAYNIEH

FOR THE KOFTAS
1kg lamb mince
2 onions, finely chopped
bunch of flat-leaf
    parsley, chopped
½ small bunch of mint,
    chopped
1 tbsp salt
1 tsp cinnamon
2 tsp Lebanese seven-
    spice mix
1 tsp allspice
1 tsp black pepper
2 tsp red pepper paste
mint leaves, to serve

FOR THE POTATOES &
    TOMATOES
2kg potatoes, peeled and
    sliced into 1cm rounds
oil, for brushing
750g medium tomatoes,
    sliced

First make the tomato sauce. Heat the oil in a medium saucepan and sauté the onion over a low heat for 10 minutes. Stir in the garlic and cook for 1–2 minutes. Add the chopped tomatoes, the tomato purée and seasoning to the pan, stir together, then pour in the stock. Bring to the boil, then simmer for 15–20 minutes on a low heat until the sauce has thickened.

Preheat the oven to 200°C/180°C fan/gas mark 6.

Next, prepare the koftas. Put all the ingredients in a bowl and mix well. You might find it easier to use your hands, rather than a spoon. Shape the mixture into 18–24 small round patties – they should all be about the same size or a little smaller than a slice of a medium tomato.

Lightly oil a couple of baking sheets and bake the koftas for 5–7 minutes. Leave the oven on to bake the whole dish once it is prepared.

Brush the sliced potatoes with oil and cook them on a lightly oiled baking sheet until just golden – about 10 minutes; they should be parcooked. Use non-stick baking parchment, if you think the potatoes may stick.

Arrange half the potatoes over the base of a large round pie dish (about 25–30cm in diameter). Then arrange half the kofta around the

1 tbsp oil

1 small onion, chopped

3 garlic cloves, crushed

4 tomatoes, skinned and chopped

2 tbsp tomato purée

2 tsp salt

1 tsp white or black pepper

1 litre chicken, lamb or beef stock

edges of the dish and put some tomato slices in the middle. Spoon tomato sauce over the top until everything is covered. Continue to layer the potatoes, koftas and tomatoes until you've used them all, finishing with a layer of sauce.

Bake in the oven for 20 minutes. Check the potatoes, tomatoes and koftas to see that they are cooked. You may need to turn the dish half way through the cooking time so the potatoes brown evenly. Scatter with a few fresh mint leaves and serve.

SERVES 6

I love lamb, aubergines and tahina — and they're even better when they're put together in a recipe such as this. By splitting baby aubergines and filling them with spiced mince you create little parcels, which are layered on top of toasted squares of flatbread and served with tender cubes of lamb, a rich tomato and lamb stock and a wonderfully creamy tahina sauce (see photo on pages 170-1). You have to keep an eye out for baby aubergines — the season is late spring and through the summer — but whenever I spot them in the shops, I snap them up to make this recipe. Served on a large platter, this looks impressive, tastes truly decadent and is really worth the effort you put into making it.

# BABY AUBERGINES WITH SPICED MINCED LAMB & TAHINA
## FATTET MAKDOUS

500g lamb fillet, cubed
2.2 litres water
2 large onions
3 garlic cloves
1kg baby aubergines
olive oil, for brushing and
    drizzling
100g butter
4 tbsp vegetable oil
250g lamb mince
1 tbsp salt
1½ tsp white or black
    pepper
1 tsp cinnamon
½ tsp Lebanese seven-
    spice mix
good pinch of allspice
2 heaped tbsp tomato
    purée
2 small flatbreads
sumac, for sprinkling
150g Greek yoghurt

Preheat the oven to 200°C/180°C fan/gas mark 6.

Put the lamb into a large pan and pour in 2 litres of the water. Chop half of one of the onions and add to the pan with 1 garlic clove. Cover with a lid and bring to a simmer. Cook, uncovered, for 30 minutes. Strain the stock into a jug and set the lamb aside.

While the lamb is simmering, prepare the aubergines. Cut a slit in each aubergine from the stalk to the end and brush with oil. Put them in a roasting tin and roast for 30 minutes until very soft. Once they're done, allow to cool a little while you prepare the minced meat stuffing.

Chop the second onion. Melt 50g of the butter in a saucepan with 1 tablespoon of the oil. Add the chopped onion and fry over a medium heat for 5 minutes. Add the minced lamb and continue to fry for a further 5 minutes. Add 2 teaspoons of the salt, 1 teaspoon of the white pepper and the spices, and stir everything together. Turn off the heat and set aside.

Chop the last onion half and finely chop a second garlic clove. Heat the remaining 3 tablespoons of olive oil in a medium saucepan and add the onion and garlic. Fry for 5 minutes over a medium heat,

100g tahina
50g pine nuts, toasted
seeds of ½ pomegranate
paprika, to season
mint leaves, to garnish

then add 1 litre of the reserved lamb stock, the tomato purée, the remaining 1 teaspoon salt and ½ teaspoon white pepper. Bring to the boil and simmer for 5–10 minutes.

Cut the flatbreads into squares (about 2–3cm). Drizzle with olive oil, sprinkle with sumac and toast under a grill. Spoon the yoghurt into a bowl and stir in the tahina. Crush and add the remaining garlic clove and stir in the remaining 150–200ml water to loosen the mixture.

Spoon 1 heaped teaspoon of the spiced mince mixture into each roasted baby aubergine. Arrange them in a roasting tin. Spoon over about three-quarters of the tomato-based stock, then bake them in the oven for 5–10 minutes.

Take a large platter – one that isn't too flat – and arrange the cubes of bread over the base. Ladle a large spoonful of stock over the top to moisten the bread, then add a large spoonful of the yoghurt dressing. Toss the bread cubes so that all the flavours mix together, then spread them out in an even layer.

Arrange the stuffed aubergines around the edge of the bread and put the lamb fillet in the middle. Spoon the rest of the yoghurt dressing over the top. Heat the remaining butter with the pine nuts and spoon over the top, followed by the pomegranate seeds, a little paprika and a few mint leaves.

**SERVES 6**

### TONY'S TIP

This recipe makes two stocks. The first, a simple lamb stock, is made by simmering tender lamb fillet. If there's any left over, cool it, then transfer it to an airtight container and freeze for up to three months. The second, the tomato-based lamb stock, is richer, but can also be frozen for up to three months. It's delicious heated up and spooned over plain rice and lamb kebabs.

I always bake extra bread cubes in the oven and keep them in an airtight container, mixed with olive oil and sumac to keep the bread crisp for longer. I then use them whenever I want, for example to sprinkle over salads.

Stuffed courgettes feature in recipes from all over the Middle East and North Africa and in parts of the Mediterranean, too. They are a canny way of making the most of a glut. This is a combination of recipes: one my grandma made for every family gathering and another from a Lebanese friend's mum, Leila. The courgettes are bathed in a light yoghurt sauce in Leila's recipe, and I love it. Make sure you choose the fattest courgettes you can find – the Lebanese ones are the slightly paler ones.

# STUFFED COURGETTES IN A YOGHURT SAUCE KOUSSA BIL LABAN

**FOR THE COURGETTES & STUFFING**

2kg medium Lebanese courgettes, ends trimmed off (the fattest you can find)
100g short grain rice, such as pudding or risotto rice
200g lamb mince
50g butter or ghee, softened
2 tsp salt
1 tsp cinnamon
1 tsp Lebanese seven-spice mix
1 tsp allspice
1 tsp black or white pepper

**FOR THE SAUCE**

1kg Greek yoghurt
500ml water
2 tbsp cornflour
1 tsp white pepper
1 tsp salt
2 tbsp butter or ghee
4 garlic cloves, crushed
1 tbsp dried mint

**SERVES 6–8**

Use a long, sharp knife with a narrow blade to cut into each courgette and remove the spongy middle that holds the seeds. Move the blade around inside and keep going until you've removed all the seeds.

Put the rice into a large bowl and add the lamb, butter, salt, cinnamon, seven-spice, allspice and pepper. Mix everything together. Use a teaspoon to spoon the mixture into each courgette, pressing it down lightly until it's about 2cm from the end.

Lay the courgettes in a large, deep saucepan and pour in enough cold water to cover. Put a plate on top of the courgettes to weight them down, then cover the pan with a lid. Bring to the boil, then turn the heat down to a medium simmer and cook for about 15–20 minutes. The courgettes should be tender and the rice cooked.

While the courgettes are simmering, put the yoghurt, water, cornflour, pepper and salt into a wide heavy-based saucepan. Put over a medium heat and bring slowly to the boil. Whisk the mixture continuously until it thickens, which will take a good 10 minutes. Don't leave it as you need to make sure it doesn't split. Turn off the heat once it's thickened.

Lift the courgettes out of the pan and drain a little, then lower them into the yoghurt sauce. Alternatively, arrange them in a dish and spoon the yoghurt sauce over them.

Melt the butter in a small frying pan and cook the garlic for about a minute until just golden. Add the dried mint, then take the pan off the heat and scatter over the yoghurt. Serve straight away.

Tender little nuggets of chickpeas bathed in a cumin-scented dressing and topped with a creamy yoghurt and tahina sauce – what's not to love about this simple but very tasty dish? Back in the day, chickpeas were considered a poor man's supper, and when I was little, instead of snacking on nuts, which were expensive, I'd have chickpeas. We even used to eat sugar-coated chickpeas as a treat. In this recipe, the method of cooking the chickpeas is just the same as for hommos. Soaking the chickpeas in bicarbonate of soda beforehand softens the pulses during cooking. It's important to drain this off and then cook them in fresh water, though, or they may end up with a soapy taste.

# CHICKPEAS WITH YOGHURT & TAHINA SAUCE
## MOUSSABAHA

200g dried chickpeas
2 tsp bicarbonate of
    soda
200g Greek yoghurt
50g tahina
3 garlic cloves, crushed
2 tsp cumin, plus extra
    to season
100ml olive oil
juice of 1 lemon
1 tsp salt
½ tomato, finely chopped
a little chopped flat-leaf
    parsley
paprika, to serve

The night before, or 8–10 hours ahead, put the dried chickpeas into a bowl, cover them in cold water and leave to soak overnight.

The next day, drain the chickpeas, add the bicarbonate of soda, then cover with cold water again. Leave to one side for 30 minutes.

Drain the chickpeas again, then tip into a medium-large saucepan and cover with cold water. Cover the pan with a lid, bring to the boil, then reduce the heat and simmer uncovered for 40 minutes.

Meanwhile, make the sauce. Mix the yoghurt and tahina in a large bowl with half the garlic. If it's very thick, add a little water to thin it down.

Drain the chickpeas and put into a bowl. Add the rest of the garlic, the cumin, 50ml of the olive oil, the lemon juice and salt. Mix everything together, making sure the chickpeas are well coated with all the seasonings, oil and lemon juice. Spoon them into the serving dish, pour the sauce over the top, and add the rest of the olive oil, the chopped tomato, the parsley and a dash of paprika and cumin to garnish.

SERVES 6

174

I remember eating this dish as a child, mopping up the juices with a big chunk of bread. I'd complain to my mum if there wasn't enough garlic in it! This finished dish is just how I like it. The recipe is made in stages, and the two parts are mixed in one big pot to bring all the flavours together. It's very good just as it is, but if you want, serve it with bread or rice.

# CHICKEN & CHICKPEA STEW
## YAKNATT DAJAJ BIL HOMMOS

**FOR THE CHICKEN**

1 large chicken, jointed into 12 pieces
50ml olive oil
5 garlic cloves, crushed
salt and black pepper
a pinch each of cinnamon and Lebanese seven-spice mix

**FOR THE STEW**

50g butter or ghee
100ml vegetable oil
1 large onion, chopped
10 garlic cloves, crushed
5 tomatoes, skinned and finely chopped
2 tbsp tomato purée
500g Chantenay carrots, peeled
2 x 400g tins chickpeas, drained and rinsed
1 tbsp cumin
2 tsp salt
1 tsp black pepper
1 litre hot chicken stock
chopped coriander, to serve

Put the chicken pieces into a roasting tin. Add the olive oil and garlic, then season generously with the salt, pepper, and the pinch each of cinnamon and Lebanese seven-spice. Toss everything together so the chicken pieces are well coated. Set aside for 30 minutes to marinate.

Preheat the oven to 200°C/180°C fan/gas mark 6. Roast the chicken pieces for 20–30 minutes.

While the chicken pieces are roasting, make the stew. Melt the butter in a large saucepan with the vegetable oil. Add the onion and garlic, and fry over a low-to-medium heat for 5–10 minutes. Add the chopped tomatoes, tomato purée, carrots, chickpeas, cumin, salt and pepper. Stir everything together to make sure the spices and seasoning are thoroughly mixed in. Pour the stock into the pan and cover with a lid. Bring to the boil, then turn the heat down low and simmer for 30 minutes.

When the chicken pieces are cooked, remove the tin from the oven, lift them out and drop them into the stew, along with any juices from the roasting tin. Cover the pan again and cook for 5–10 minutes over a low heat. Now you're done.

Spoon into bowls, garnish with a little fresh coriander and serve.

**SERVES 6**

When I first came to London I discovered shepherd's pie, which reminded me of this recipe that my mum used to make for us all. Instead of an equal layer of mince and mashed potato, this uses more mashed potato and sandwiches a thin filling of spiced mince between two layers of it. The mash and mince are seasoned and lightly spiced with the same ingredients, which brings together all the flavours beautifully. This rich dish needs something light and zingy on the side. I like to serve it with Village Tomato Salad, which cuts through it perfectly.

# POTATO & SPICED MINCED LAMB PIE KIBET BATATA BIL SAYNIEH

150g fine wholewheat
   bulgar wheat
3 onions
2kg potatoes, cut into
   chunks
75g butter or ghee
75ml vegetable oil
200g lamb mince
100g pine nuts, toasted
2 tsp cumin
2 tsp cinnamon
2 tsp Lebanese seven-
   spice mix
2 tbsp salt
1 tsp white pepper
100g breadcrumbs

TO SERVE
tahina, to drizzle
small handful of chopped
   flat-leaf parsley
handful of toasted
   pine nuts
cinnamon, for sprinkling

Put the bulgar wheat in a bowl, just cover with water and soak for 15 minutes. Cut one onion in half, and grate the half, squeezing out any excess juice. Set the other half aside.

Put the potatoes in a large saucepan, cover with water and a lid, and bring to the boil. Simmer for 15 minutes until soft.

Preheat the oven to 200°C/180°C fan/gas mark 6.

While the potatoes are cooking, chop the remaining onions, melt 50g of the butter in a frying pan with 50ml of the oil then cook the onions over a medium heat for about 10 minutes. Add the lamb and continue to cook for 5 minutes. Add the pine nuts, 1 teaspoon each of the cumin, cinnamon, Lebanese seven-spice mix and 1 tablespoon of the salt. Mix well.

Drain the potatoes then tip them back into the pan to dry. Mash, then add the bulgar wheat, the grated onion and the remaining spices and salt and pepper. Mash everything together so it's really smooth.

Spread most of the remaining butter and oil over a large ovenproof dish. Tip half the breadcrumbs over the base and spread them out. Tip away any that don't stick.

Take half the mash and spread it over the base, then wet your hands and flatten the potato. Drain the meat mixture of any fat or juices, then spoon over the top. Spread the remaining potato on top and again flatten it with your hands. Make a diamond pattern with a fork on top, pressing down gently on the mash.

Spread with the remaining oil and butter. Cover with the remaining breadcrumbs, and again tip away any excess crumbs.

Bake in the oven for about 30 minutes until the top is golden. Drizzle over the tahina, scatter with parsley and a generous handful of toasted pine nuts, and sprinkle with cinnamon to serve.

**SERVES 6–8**

Crunchy, nutty, earthy, wholesome and hearty, these recipes are a mix of all that is wonderful about Middle Eastern cooking: ancient grains, an abundance of fresh vegetables, juicy chicken and lamb, and layers of herbs and spices. I grew up in a house that always had grains and pulses in the cupboard – largely we bought 10g bags!

# GRAINS & PULSES

You can see why stuffed peppers are popular all over the Middle East, North Africa and in the Mediterranean, too. It's a handy and cheap way of making the most of this vegetable that you see piled high on the stands in food markets.

This recipe is pretty healthy and features a simple one-mix filling. The peppers are left to bake in the oven until they are tender and the rice is cooked. When I'm choosing the peppers, I make sure I pick good-size ones that will take a generous amount of filling. I tend to use a teaspoon to spoon in the rice mixture so I can tuck all the bits down into the corners of the base of the peppers and make the most of the space inside.

# STUFFED PEPPERS WITH SPICED RICE & LAMB MAHSHY FELFEL

6–8 large, mixed colour
 peppers
1 tbsp olive oil
1 garlic clove, crushed
salt and black pepper

FOR THE FILLING
150g short grain rice,
 such as Arborio
4 tomatoes, chopped
1 small onion, chopped
1 small fennel bulb,
 chopped
2 garlic cloves, crushed
small bunch of flat-leaf
 parsley, chopped
200ml tomato juice
½ tbsp Lebanese seven-
 spice mix
1 tsp salt
1 tsp black pepper
2 tbsp lemon juice

Preheat the oven to 200°C/180°C fan/gas mark 6.

Put all the ingredients for the filling into a large bowl and stir everything together. Rest a sieve over a bowl and spoon the filling into it, then set aside to drain.

Prepare the peppers. Cut off the lids by slicing around each pepper about 1cm down from the stalk. Use a small sharp knife to loosen the filaments and knock out the seeds. Throw these away. Brush the insides of each with oil and the garlic, then season.

Spoon the drained filling into the hollowed-out peppers and put them in an ovenproof dish or roasting tin, making sure they fit quite tightly, with just a little bit of space around each one.

Spoon any cooking juices over the top. Cover the dish or tin with foil and cook in the oven for 1 hour–1 hour 20 minutes, until the rice is cooked and the peppers are tender.

SERVES 6–8

Maklouba, a famous dish in Palestine, means 'upside down' and whenever I'm invited for a meal at my Palestinian friends' home they make this. Even this simplified version is deilcious and looks very impressive.

# PALESTINIAN SPICED RICE WITH CHICKEN MAKLOUBA

1 chicken, jointed into 8 pieces
2 tsp salt, plus 1 tbsp
1 tsp cinnamon
1 tsp Lebanese seven-spice mix
3 tbsp ghee or butter
50ml olive oil, plus extra for roasting and frying
3 onions
3 litres hot water
1kg aubergines, half sliced and half chopped
1 red pepper, halved, deseeded and chopped into 3cm squares
500g basmati rice

TO SERVE
50g nuts, including roasted almonds, toasted pine nuts and slivered pistachio nuts
small handful of flat-leaf parsley leaves, chopped
200g Greek yoghurt, seasoned and mixed with ¼ chopped cucumber

Preheat the oven to 200°C/180°C fan/gas mark 6. Put the chicken pieces in a roasting tin and add the salt, cinnamon and seven-spice mix, then mix with the ghee and 1 tablespoon of oil. Roast in the oven for 15 minutes until the chicken is just golden.

Slice two of the onions, then heat 50ml oil in a large, deep saucepan and fry for 10-15 minutes over a medium heat until dark golden. Add the hot water to the pan, then the chicken pieces. Simmer for 30 minutes, covered, until they are very tender.

Heat a tablespoon of oil in a large frying pan and fry the aubergine slices over a medium heat in batches, until golden. Set aside on a plate, then fry the chopped aubergine and pepper.

About 10 minutes before the chicken is ready, prepare the rice. Chop the remaining onion and fry in a pan with 2 tablespoons each ghee and oil until golden. Stir in the rice, along with 1 tablespoon salt.

Lift the chicken pieces out of the pan and set aside to keep warm.

Stir 1 litre chicken stock into the rice. Spoon the chopped aubergines and pepper on top, cover the pan and cook on the lowest heat until the rice is cooked – about 10 minutes; all the water should be absorbed.

This is what I do to serve: arrange the fried aubergine slices, overlapping, on the base of a large pan. Layer the cooked rice and vegetable mixture with the chicken pieces on top, then press down. You may need to put this in a heated oven to keep it warm.

Next, turn a large plate upside down over the pan. Holding on to the plate and the pan, carefully turn the pan over so that everything turns out on to the plate. You may need to rearrange some elements to neaten them up. Scatter the nuts and parsley over the top and serve with the yoghurt and cucumber sauce.

SERVES 6–8

This delicious Lebanese village salad is made with rice, lentils and fried onions. I love anything with fried onions on top as it adds an extra layer of flavour. This recipe contains comparatively little rice, but I really like the subtle texture it provides. Folding in a diced tomato – pick one that's really juicy and ripe – as well as chopped spring onions and mint at the end makes this taste very fresh, too.

# GREEN LENTIL & RICE SALAD
## MOUDARDARA

2 tbsp oil, plus extra for frying
1 medium onion, chopped
1 garlic clove, crushed
300g green lentils
1.2 litres hot water
50g basmati or long grain rice
½ tbsp cumin
1 tbsp salt
¼ aubergine, cut into cubes
1 tomato, diced
3 spring onions, chopped
¼ bunch of mint, finely chopped

TO SERVE
sunflower oil, for deep-frying
1 onion, thinly sliced

Heat the oil in a large saucepan over a low heat. Sauté the onion and garlic over a low heat for 10 minutes. Add the lentils and the hot water. Cover with a lid to bring to the boil then reduce the heat to very low and simmer for about 15 minutes. Stir in the rice – the lentils should be three quarters cooked by this stage – and the cumin and salt.

Replace the lid on the pan and continue to cook on a low heat for 10–15 minutes. Keep testing the rice every 5 minutes or so, as you don't want it to be overcooked.

Meanwhile, cook the crispy onions for the garnish. Pour enough sunflower oil into a medium saucepan to come about 5cm up the side and warm over a medium heat until a piece of onion sizzles in the oil. Carefully lower half the onion slices into the oil and cook until golden. Spread out on kitchen paper to drain while you cook the remainder.

Heat a little oil in a frying pan and fry the aubergine cubes until golden.

Fluff up the lentil and rice mixture with a fork – the liquid should all have been absorbed during cooking – and stir in the aubergine, tomatoes, chopped spring onions and mint.

To serve, top with the crispy onions.

**SERVES 6–8**

Burghul or bulgar wheat, as it's known here, is eaten all over the Middle East. I've tried it with chicken, with lamb, with vegetables. and in a salad, too. Highly seasoned, with lots of flavour, this recipe is a real crowd-pleaser.

# BULGAR WHEAT WITH CHICKEN
## BURGHUL BIL DAJAJ

sunflower oil, for frying
2 aubergines, chopped
  into cubes
500g coarse brown
  bulgar wheat
500ml cold water
1 small onion, chopped
1 garlic clove, crushed
2 tbsp cinnamon
1 tbsp Lebanese seven-
  spice mix
1 tsp salt
½ tbsp black pepper
5 tomatoes, chopped
2 tbsp tomato purée
500ml tomato juice
500ml chicken stock
150g tinned, drained
  chickpeas
6 skinless chicken
  thighs, bone in
3 tbsp olive or vegetable
  oil
150ml hot water

Start by frying the aubergine until golden. Heat about 2cm oil in a medium sauté pan for a couple of minutes. To check it's hot enough, add a cube of aubergine; if it sizzles, it's ready. Depending on how big your pan is, put a quarter or half of the chopped aubergine into the pan and fry until golden. Drain on kitchen paper. Continue until all the aubergine is cooked. Set aside.

Put the bulgar wheat into a bowl and cover with the cold water. Leave to soak.

Preheat the oven to 190°C/170°C fan/gas mark 5.

Heat 2 tablespoons of oil in the pan and sauté the onion and garlic over a low heat for 10 minutes. Stir in three quarters of the spices and half the salt and pepper, and cook for 1–2 minutes. Stir in the chopped tomato and cook for a further 5 minutes until it has cooked down and softened, and the mixture looks like a sauce.

Add the tomato purée and pour in the tomato juice and stock. Season, add the bulgar wheat and mix everything together, then add the chickpeas. Cover the pan with a lid and cook for 20–25 minutes over a very low heat.

Put the chicken into a roasting tin and season with the remaining spices, salt and pepper. Add 1 tablespoon of oil and toss to coat the thighs in the seasonings. Roast in the oven for about 10 minutes, until they're starting to turn golden, then reduce the heat to 170°C/150°C fan/gas mark 3.

Pour the hot water into the tin, cover the whole thing with foil and continue to roast for 15–20 minutes, until tender.

Check the bulgar wheat is cooked, then fold in the chopped aubergine and serve with the chicken.

SERVES 6

I discovered this recipe several years ago in a small village just outside Damascus. I think of it as a hearty village dish and when I described it to our Syrian chef, Wassim, he knew it. He promised to cook it for me from a recipe his mother had passed on. I was so surprised by how simple it was to do – you make a sort-of pastry by mincing lamb with fine cracked wheat and other ingredients. This is divided into two layers, then baked in the oven with a lamb mince filling. It's a great recipe to make if you have lots of friends coming as it can be made ahead then reheated. The yoghurt, mint and cucumber sauce on the side is a must, too, as it offsets the richness of the lamb.

# BULGAR WHEAT & SPICED MINCED LAMB PIE KIBBE SAYNIEH

## FOR THE FILLING
2 tbsp olive oil, plus extra for brushing
1 small onion, finely chopped
1 garlic clove, crushed
250g lamb mince
1 tsp salt
½ tbsp black pepper
½ tbsp Lebanese seven-spice mix
2 tbsp pomegranate molasses

## FOR THE DOUGH
350g fine brown bulgar wheat
225ml water
1 small onion, roughly chopped
leaves from ¾ bunch of mint
1 tsp salt
½ tbsp black pepper
½ tbsp cinnamon

To make the filling heat the olive oil in a saucepan and sauté the onion and garlic over a medium heat, stirring, for 5–10 minutes. Stir in the lamb, seasoning, seven-spice and molasses, then turn the heat low and simmer for 20 minutes. Set aside to cool.

To make the bottom and top dough layers, put the cracked wheat in a bowl and add 100ml of the water to moisten it.

Put the onion into a food processor and add the mint leaves. Whizz to chop the onion into smaller pieces. Add the salt, pepper, cinnamon, meat, bulgar wheat and the ice. Cover with the lid and with the motor on low, slowly add the remaining 125ml water until the dough becomes smooth. It should feel like bread dough and be pliable, as if you could roll it.

Preheat the oven to 170°C/150°C fan/gas mark 3.

Oil a large, flat, round dish, about 28cm diameter. Divide the mixture in half and shape half into a round. Put it on a piece of cling film, then cover it with another piece of cling film. Roll the dough out thinly to fit the base of the dish, then lift off the cling film and put the dough in the dish. Trim the edges. This layer needs to be slightly thinner than the top so the base will be crispy at the edges once baked.

500g lean lamb fillet or leg, minced
5–6 ice cubes
4 medium tomatoes on the vine, each sliced into 6–8 wedges

FOR THE CUCUMBER & YOGHURT SAUCE
200g Greek yoghurt
½ cucumber, chopped
2 garlic cloves, crushed
2–3 tbsp tahina
pinch of dried mint, plus extra to garnish
salt, to taste

TO SERVE
sumac, for sprinkling
extra-virgin olive oil for drizzling
25g pine nuts, toasted
sprig of mint

Spread the cooled filling over the top. Roll out the other piece of dough, again between two sheets of cling film. Place on top of the filling. Drizzle the top with olive oil and score into a diamond pattern with a sharp knife. Arrange the tomato wedges around the edges.

Bake in the oven for 40–50 minutes or until golden on top.

Mix the yoghurt, cucumber, garlic and tahina together in a bowl. Spoon into a serving bowl, sprinkle with dried mint and garnish with extra mint.

To serve, sprinkle the tomatoes with sumac and drizzle with a little extra-virgin olive oil. Garnish with pine nuts and mint leaves, and serve, cut into wedges, with the sauce.

**SERVES 6–8**

I have fond memories of Swiss chard from when I was little and my grandmother would cook it in a stew with olive oil and garlic for my grandad. It was his favourite dish. This recipe for stuffing the leaves with rice is one I enjoyed with an Iraqi family. The seasoning of Lebanese seven-spice mix and an additional touch of mint, is, I think, what makes this taste so delicious. (See photo on pages 192-3.)

The cooking time of different brands and types of rice varies, so I check that they're done (because you really don't want overcooked soggy parcels) by picking out a parcel and unwrapping it a little. Take a grain of rice and bite it — if it's just tender, they're ready. If you taste a grain and it seems to be almost there, you can turn off the heat and leave the parcels in the pan with the lid on for 5-10 minutes to finish cooking.

# STUFFED SWISS CHARD WITH SPICED RICE & VEGETABLES
## MAHSHI SELEK

1–1.2kg Swiss chard leaves, woody stalks trimmed
1–2 potatoes, sliced
2–3 large tomatoes, sliced
2 medium onions, sliced
3 garlic cloves, sliced
black pepper

FOR THE FILLING
250g pudding or short grain rice, such as Arborio
3 ripe tomatoes, diced
1 medium onion, finely chopped
bunch of flat-leaf parsley, chopped

Prepare the filling first. Put the rice, tomatoes, onion, parsley, mint, lemon juice, salt, spice mix and olive oil into a bowl. Give the mixture a good stir, then put the bowl to one side to marinate for about 20 minutes to allow the juices to develop.

Bring a large saucepan of water to the boil and fill a large bowl with water and ice (for a water bath). Throw a good pinch of salt into the pan. Blanch the chard leaves in batches, by dipping each leaf in the boiling water, pulling it out and then dipping it in the water bath to cool down quickly. Don't leave the leaves in the boiling water for too long or they'll overcook and become too delicate to work with when you're stuffing them. Lay them on a clean tea towel to drain well.

Rest a sieve over a bowl and spoon the filling into it to drain the juices into the bowl. Take a wooden spoon and press down with the back to extract all the juices, reserving them.

Take a blanched leaf and lay it on a board with the stalk away from you. Spoon ½–1 tablespoon of the filling into the top third nearest

bunch of mint, chopped
juice of 2 lemons
1½ tbsp salt, plus extra
for seasoning
1 tbsp Lebanese seven-
spice mix
75–100ml olive oil

1 large tomato, halved,
deseeded and finely
chopped
1 mild red chilli, halved,
deseeded and finely
chopped

you, fold over the bottom, roll a little, then fold in the sides. Now you have the beginnings of a little parcel, continue to roll it up tightly, as if you're making a spring roll, tucking the other end under once you've finished rolling. Do the same with all the leaves until they're full and you've used all the filling.

In a large, wide sauté pan, layer the potatoes, tomatoes, onions and garlic, seasoning each layer. Arrange the chard parcels on top, tucking them in neatly next to each other.

Measure the drained juices in a jug and top up with water to 1 litre. Pour this over the parcels, then cover with a plate just large enough to fit over the top and weight it down. Cover the pan with a lid and bring to the boil. Turn the heat down and simmer for about 1 hour. Start checking after about 30–35 minutes to see whether the rice is cooked.

Arrange the parcels on a plate, spoon the potato, tomato and onion into the middle, and garnish with chopped tomato and chilli.

**SERVES 6–8**

Freekeh has a nutty taste and is a good match for chicken or lamb and delicious in salads. This recipe comes via the aunt of my Palestinian friend Haleem. Her name is Um-Omar, and she made it for me in Jordan. You need to check the cooking time of your freekeh, as it varies. Taste as you go, adding more stock, if necessary, so that it's just the way you like it.

# FREEKEH WITH CHICKEN
## FREKEH BIL DAJAJ

500g freekeh
8 chicken thighs
2 tsp salt
1 tsp black pepper
1 tsp cinnamon
1 tsp Lebanese seven-
    spice mix
1 tsp allspice
100g butter or ghee
50ml vegetable oil
1½ onions, very finely
    chopped
1 carrot, chopped
1 bay leaf

FOR THE SAUCE
200g Greek yoghurt
3-4 mini cucumbers,
    grated
1 garlic clove, crushed
    with a pinch of salt
1 tsp dried mint

TO SERVE
50g pine nuts, roasted
50g flaked almonds,
    roasted

Preheat the oven to 220°C/200°C fan/gas mark 7. Wash the freekeh in cold water, add to a bowl, cover with hot water and soak for 1 hour.

Next marinate the chicken. Mix 1 teaspoon salt, ½ teaspoon pepper, cinnamon, ½ teaspoon seven-spice, ½ teaspoon allspice, 50g butter and 25ml vegetable oil in a bowl. Pour over the chicken in a roasting tin, then brown in the oven for 20 minutes.

Take the tin out of the oven. Put the contents in a large saucepan and pour over enough hot water to cover. Add two-thirds of the onion, the carrot and the bay leaf to flavour the stock. Cover, bring to the boil and simmer for 30 minutes so that it's really tender. Strain and reserve the liquid and use as stock to cook the freekeh.

Preheat the oven to 100°C/80°C fan/gas mark ¼. Put the chicken in a roasting tin with a little hot water at the bottom and cover with foil to keep warm while you cook the freekeh. If your freekeh takes about 1 hour to cook, put the chicken in the oven to reheat about half an hour before the freekeh is ready.

Heat the rest of the butter or ghee in a large casserole and sauté the remaining chopped onion over a medium heat until golden – about 5-7 minutes. Drain the freekeh and add to the pan plus the remaining salt, pepper and spices. Stir everything well and pour in 500ml of the reserved stock. Simmer over a low heat and keep an eye on it. It will take 30 minutes-1 hour, depending on which brand you buy. Keep adding more stock, if the freekeh looks dry. Once it's cooked and tender, cover and leave to rest for 10 minutes.

Mix all the sauce ingredients in a bowl and serve alongside the chicken and freekeh, with the nuts scattered over the top.

SERVES 6-8

The first time I ate this was at the home of a farmer, Abu Zaki, who I'd met in a food market south of Lebanon, where he was selling his produce. As we chatted about seasonal fruits and vegetables, he invited me to meet his family, and it was then that he prepared this for me. That is a bit of a one-off in Middle Eastern culture as the kitchen tends to be the wife's domain.

The tomatoes have to be really ripe and very juicy for this recipe as it's their juices that soften and moisten the fine brown bulgar wheat. We serve it as part of a mezze with lots of other little dishes before the main course, but I eat it at any time of day as it's so nourishing with all those lovely herbs and vegetables.

# BULGAR WHEAT & TOMATO SALAD
## KIBBE BANADOURA

150g fine brown bulgar
wheat
3 ripe beef tomatoes,
finely chopped
1 bunch of spring onions,
finely chopped
¼ bunch of mint,
chopped, plus extra to
garnish
¼ bunch of basil,
chopped
¼ red chilli, finely
chopped
½ tbsp salt
½ tbsp cumin
25ml extra-virgin
olive oil

Put the bulgar wheat in a bowl and add enough water to cover it. Leave to one side for 15 minutes to soak, then drain.

Put the tomatoes, and any juice on the board from chopping them, into a large bowl. Add the spring onions, the soaked bulgar wheat, mint, basil, most of the chilli, the salt, cumin and olive oil.

Stir everything together, cover and set aside for 30 minutes. During this time the bulgar wheat will soften as it soaks up the juice from the tomatoes and the olive oil.

Spoon into a serving bowl, scatter over the extra mint and remaining chilli, and serve.

**SERVES 6–8 GENEROUSLY**

This recipe is one I enjoyed in Jordan at my friend Jamal's grandmother's house, which reminded me how much we love stuffing vegetables in the Middle East. She made it for us with beautifully cooked, tender lamb cutlets arranged on a large platter, and I particularly loved the flavours of lemon, fried garlic and mint added at the end.

# STUFFED CABBAGE LEAVES WITH SPICED MINCED LAMB & RICE
## MAHSHI MALFOUF

1 heavy Lebanese or flat head cabbage, leaves separated from the stalk and trimmed
200g lamb mince
150g pudding rice
3 tbsp butter or ghee
½ tsp cinnamon, plus extra to season
½ tsp Lebanese seven-spice mix, plus extra to season
½ tsp black pepper, plus extra to season
1 tsp salt, plus extra to season
12 lamb cutlets (about 1kg)
1 litre beef, lamb or chicken stock
5 garlic cloves, sliced
1 tbsp dried mint
juice of 2 lemons
mint leaves, to serve

Depending on the size of the cabbage, use halved leaves or whole, smaller leaves. Bring a large saucepan of water to the boil and simmer the leaves for 3–5 minutes, then drain and plunge into a bowl of cold water to stop them cooking. Drain again and cool. Cut out the ribs.

In a medium bowl mix the mince, rice, 1 tablespoon butter, cinnamon, seven-spice, black pepper and salt. Put 1 large tablespoon of the filling into a cabbage leaf and roll up. Trim the ends. Don't put in too much filling or the rice will expand and fall out of the sides. Continue until you've used all the mixture and made about 18 rolls.

Season the cutlets with salt, pepper, cinnamon and a little seven-spice. Heat a splash of oil in a frying pan and brown them on both sides. Arrange them over the base of a large, deep saucepan, cover with any leftover cabbage leaves and top with the rolled-up cabbage parcels.

Put a plate on top and then something heavy on top of the plate. Pour the stock over the top, cover with a lid, bring to the boil and turn the heat down. Simmer for 30–45 minutes, until the rice is cooked.

Heat the remaining butter in a small frying pan and fry the garlic until just golden. Add the mint, then remove from the heat. When the cabbage parcels are cooked, drizzle over the remaining butter and the lemon juice, and simmer for a further 3–5 minutes.

Allow to cool for 10–15 minutes. Either arrange the cutlets and parcels on a large plate to serve, or turn everything out together. If you're going to do this, strain off and discard the stock, then put a platter over the saucepan and turn it over. Make sure you do this over a sink.

SERVES 6

Giant Lebanese couscous, also known as moghrabieh, forms the base of this dish. It's totally different in taste and texture from the fine couscous we use in other dishes. Chunky, with a slightly firm bite, it works perfectly with the other main ingredients used here: chicken, baby onions and chickpeas (see photo on pages 202-3). My mum used to make it for the family, and at home we would eat it from a very large dish. We'd gather round the table, and Mum would push in nine spoons and we'd all eat from the dish. It was a lovely way of bringing us together as a family.

# GIANT COUSCOUS WITH CHICKEN
## MOUGHARABIEH DAJAJ

### FOR THE STOCK
vegetable oil, for frying
500g lamb shank, meat cut off the bone in 2.5cm pieces
2 litres water
1 onion, halved
2 bay leaves
2 cinnamon sticks

### FOR THE STEW
12 chicken drumsticks
25g ground caraway
25g ground cinnamon, plus extra to garnish
3 tsp salt
1 tsp black pepper
100g ghee, plus a little extra for frying
1 tbsp vegetable oil, plus a little extra
500g baby onions, peeled
2 x 400g tins chickpeas, drained
2 tbsp cornflour
1kg giant couscous or moghrabieh
chopped flat-leaf parsley, to garnish

Preheat the oven to 220°C/200°C fan/gas mark 7.

To make the stock, heat a little vegetable oil in a large saucepan, add the lamb pieces and fry for 5 minutes to brown. Pour in the water, cover with a lid and bring to the boil. Then add the halved onion, bay leaves and cinnamon sticks. Turn the heat down and simmer for 1 hour until tender.

For the stew, put the drumsticks in a large roasting tin. Sprinkle over ½ teaspoon caraway and ½ teaspoon cinnamon, 1 teaspoon salt, ½ teaspoon black pepper and 25g of the ghee. Mix everything together and roast for 25 minutes until golden.

In a large frying pan heat 1 tablespoon oil until hot. Add the baby onions and cook until golden brown - they should still be quite firm at this stage. Set aside.

When the stock is ready and the meat tender, take a large, clean saucepan and pour 1 litre of the stock into it. Add half the remaining caraway and cinnamon, 1 teaspoon salt, ½ teaspoon pepper, and whisk together. Bring to the boil.

Add half the chickpeas, half the baby onions and the drumsticks. Cover and simmer over a low heat for 15-20 minutes. Add the lamb, too, and simmer for 5 minutes.

Put the cornflour into a small bowl and stir in 3 tablespoons cold water. Pour into the saucepan and simmer for a few minutes more. Taste to check the seasoning.

Cook the giant couscous in a steamer for 30–45 minutes, or according to the instructions on the packet. Keep the pan covered, but stir the couscous every now and then so that it cooks evenly. Steam until it is just tender, but still has a slight bite, so it doesn't overcook at the next stage.

Add the remaining ghee and the couscous to the saucepan, along with the rest of the caraway and cinnamon and 1 teaspoon of salt, then stir it all together and cook for 1 minute.

Use a ladle to add a little more stock to the saucepan, spooning it over the top. Add the remaining chickpeas and simmer to allow the flavours to meld together, stirring gently every now and again. Heat a little oil and a knob of ghee in a frying pan and add the remaining baby onions. Cook over a medium heat until caramelised. Season well.

Transfer the couscous mixture to a bowl, place the chicken pieces around the edge, and spoon the caramelised baby onions and chickpeas on top. To finish, break the cinnamon stick into small shards and scatter a few over the top with a good pinch of extra cinnamon and the parsley.

**SERVES 6**

No feast is complete without something sweet to finish on. Desserts are my biggest weakness – once I start I don't stop until it's all gone! Drinks add another flavour dimension to what you're eating, so experiment with them and see what you like the best.

# DESSERTS & DRINKS

I often describe this pudding to my non-Arab friends as Lebanese millefeuille because of its sweet, crunchy pastry encasing a rich, creamy cheese filling, all bathed in a decadent orange-blossom syrup. The eye-catching dessert is a sight to behold when you see it freshly made in different bakeries in Palestine, Syria, Jordan and Lebanon. Kunefe is always served warm, so if you have any left over and want to eat it the next day, warm it in the microwave so the cheese is melting and warm.

# SHREDDED FILO & CHEESE PUDDING WITH A ROSE-HONEY SYRUP KUNEFE

butter, to grease
100g cornflour
5g gum mastic
300ml double cream
250g akawi cheese, washed (or grated mozzarella)
25g pistachio nuts, finely chopped, to decorate

FOR THE DOUGH
500g shredded filo pastry
3 tbsp butter
1–2 tbsp powdered red food colouring

FOR THE SYRUP
500g granulated sugar
1.1 litres water
zest of 1 lemon
3 tbsp orange blossom water or rose water

Preheat the oven to 200°C/180°C fan/gas mark 6. Grease a 25cm springform cake tin with a little butter.

First, make the syrup. Put the sugar and 1 litre of the water into a saucepan with the lemon zest. Bring to the boil and simmer for 10 minutes. Cool, then stir in the orange blossom or rose water. Set aside.

Next make the cream mixture. Mix the cornflour with 100ml water in a measuring jug, then stir in the gum mastic. Bring the cream slowly to the boil and, once boiling, slowly pour in the cornflour mixture. Take the pan off the heat and whisk well. Cool a little.

To prepare the dough, put the shredded filo into a food processor and whizz to break it up until the strands look like grains of rice. You can do this in two batches, if it's easier. Tip into a bowl and add the butter. Rub this in with your fingers, then sprinkle over the food colouring and rub this in, too (use food gloves, if you don't want to stain your hands). Keep working the dough until it is an even colour all over.

Put half the dough into the cake tin and level the surface. Spoon the cream mixture on top, followed by the cheese and spread it out. Spoon the rest of the dough mixture on top of that and level with the back of a spoon.

Bake in the oven for about 1 hour until golden. Put the cake tin on a baking tray and spoon the syrup over the top, whipping out any lemon zest if it's about to fall on top of the cake. Scatter the pistachios over the top and serve.

SERVES 12

208

I discovered cheesecake when I moved to London, in 1988, in one of my first jobs, washing up and cleaning in a bakery run by a lovely Turkish family on the Walworth Road in Elephant and Castle. I hold very fond memories of working there, and I still pop in whenever I'm passing through south London. This cheesecake uses dark chocolate, tahina and pistachios, all marbled together and spooned on top of a classic digestive-biscuit base. It's a match made in heaven. (See photo on page 210.)

# TAHINA, CHOCOLATE & PISTACHIO CHEESECAKE

**FOR THE BASE**
150g digestive biscuits
50g pistachio nuts, toasted
125g butter, plus a little extra for greasing

**FOR THE TOPPING**
250g dark chocolate (70% cocoa solids)
25g butter
250ml double cream
50g runny honey
100g tahina
75g icing sugar
zest of 1 orange
600g mascarpone cheese
1 tbsp vanilla extract
250g cream cheese

**TO SERVE**
25g pistachio nuts, chopped
halva, crumbled
toasted sesame seeds

Grease and line a circular 20–24cm springform tin with some baking parchment.

Whizz the biscuits and pistachios in a food processor until the biscuits have become crumbs and the pistachios are finely chopped. Melt the butter in a medium saucepan over a low heat. Tip the crushed biscuits into the pan, stir together, then tip everything into the prepared tin. Level it with the back of a spoon and chill.

Now prepare the marbled topping. Break up the chocolate and put in a large, heatproof bowl. Add the butter, 100ml of the cream, the honey and tahina. Place over a pan of just-simmering water and leave for 5–10 minutes until the chocolate and butter have melted. Take a spoon and very gently stir everything together.

Meanwhile, put the rest of the cream, the icing sugar, orange zest, mascarpone, vanilla extract and cream cheese in a large bowl. Fold them together.

Take the melted chocolate mixture and drizzle it over the cream mixture, folding everything together until you have a marbled mixture. Spoon into the chilled cake tin, level the top and chill for 4 hours until set.

Loosen the tin and take off the paper around the edge. Slide a large fish slice under the cheesecake to loosen it and put it on a serving plate. Scatter the pistachio nuts, halva and toasted sesame seeds over the top and serve.

**SERVES 12**

**DESSERTS & DRINKS**

Pomegranates are one of my must-have fruits. I used to pick them from trees in my uncles' and grandparents' garden on a hot summer's day. I would open them and eat them seed by seed, sharing them with my cousins and brothers. So I just had to use the fruit in a dessert for this book. To serve, I like to pour the sauce dramatically over the top, but if you don't have a plate big enough, just pour over half the sauce, and serve the rest in a jug on the side (see photo on page 211).

# POMEGRANATE & PISTACHIO CHEESECAKE

**FOR THE BASE**
225g digestive biscuits
50g pistachio nuts, toasted
100g butter, plus extra to grease

**FOR THE FILLING**
1.25kg cream cheese
340g caster sugar
2 tsp vanilla extract
5 medium eggs

**FOR THE TOPPING**
200ml pomegranate juice
100g caster sugar
15g powdered pectin
1 pomegranate

Preheat the oven to 210°C/190°C fan/gas mark 7. Grease and line a 25cm loose-bottomed or springform cake tin with baking parchment.

Whizz the biscuits and pistachios in a food processor until finely ground. Melt the butter in a medium saucepan over a very low heat. Tip in the biscuit mixture and stir together – it'll go from being dry crumbs to looking a bit greasy and will start to clump together once all the butter is mixed in.

Spoon into the cake tin and even out the surface using the back of a spoon to press down on the mixture and make it smooth. Bake for 10 minutes. Take out of the oven and leave to cool.

Spoon the cream cheese into a large bowl. Add the sugar and mix briefly, then add the vanilla and eggs. Whisk quickly until smooth with an electric hand whisk.

Pour the mixture into the cake tin, then shake the tin to level the surface. Put in the oven and bake for 20–30 minutes.

Leave in the oven to cool overnight.

The next day, make the topping. Pour the pomegranate juice, sugar and pectin into a saucepan and bring to the boil. Turn off the heat and cool.

Take the cheesecake out of the tin. Put it on a board or large plate and spoon some sauce over it. Separate the pomegranate seeds, then scatter over the top and spoon more sauce over the top. Serve.

**SERVES 12**

This is popular in the Lebanon and throughout the Middle East and is the equivalent of the Italian dessert panna cotta. There's no gelatine in it, though, so vegetarians can eat it, too. I used to think of it as a babies' pudding – it's like nursery food because the texture is so smooth, silky and easy to eat. It's often made with orange blossom water, but I wanted to serve this recipe with some of my favourite summer berries, scented with a few drops of rose water.

# ROSE MOUHALABIAH WITH SUMMER FRUIT COMPOTE

750ml milk
175g granulated sugar
75ml double cream
100g cornflour, mixed
   with 125ml water
5g gum mastic
3 tbsp rose water

FOR THE FRUIT COMPOTE
75g caster sugar
15g powdered pectin, or
   60ml liquid pectin
50ml orange juice
2 tbsp rose water
150g strawberries,
   halved or quartered
150g blueberries
100g raspberries
100g yellow raspberries
rose petals, to decorate

You will need 6 x 175ml
   mouhalabiah cups or
   dariole moulds

Pour the milk into a saucepan and bring to the boil. Add the sugar, cream, cornflour mixture and gum mastic. As soon as the mixture starts boiling, turn off the heat and stir in the rose water.

Divide evenly among the six mouhalabiah cups. Set aside to cool, then put them in the fridge to set.

Next, make the compote. Put the sugar, pectin, orange juice and rose water into a medium saucepan. Cook over a low heat until the sugar and pectin dissolve. Add the strawberries and cook for 1–2 minutes to soften, then add the blueberries, and again cook for about 1 minute. Finally, add the raspberries, gently coat them in the syrup then turn off the heat. The fruit should not be too cooked. Leave to cool.

When you're ready to serve, turn each mouhalabiya out on to a plate. Spoon over the cooled compote and scatter with rose petals.

SERVES 6

I first discovered this delicious pudding at the home of my Egyptian friends, Amr and his wife Olympia, in Cairo. All I remember is that, full as I was, I still couldn't resist more than one helping, and I made sure I didn't leave the house without knowing how to make it. Since then, whenever I visit they'll serve it and sometimes even send some in a special refrigerated parcel, via one of our friends visiting London. I love the way the sultanas are studded throughout, providing a little bit of texture in the creaminess, while the cinnamon softens the sweetness of the sweet potato.

# SWEET POTATO & TAHINA PUDDING
## BATATA HELWA BIL TAHINA

125g sultanas
1 tsp cinnamon, plus extra to sprinkle
4 tbsp honey
500g sweet potato, chopped into chunks
50g butter
50g plain flour
250ml milk
500ml double cream
2 tbsp tahina
100g caster sugar
toasted sesame seeds, to serve

Put the sultanas into a small saucepan and pour in enough water to cover. Add the cinnamon and the honey, cover with a lid and bring to a simmer. Cook for 5 minutes. Leave to cool.

Steam the sweet potato until tender, then mash until smooth.

While the sweet potato is steaming, melt the butter in a large saucepan over a low heat and add the flour. Stir for at least 1 minute, until the flour and butter turns into a paste and starts to leave the sides of the pan.

Gradually add the milk to the pan, stirring continuously, then the cream, tahina and sugar, and stir well over a low heat until the mixture is smooth.

Mix in the mashed sweet potato, half the sultanas and stir until smooth. Pour into a large serving dish or individual glasses and cool, then chill. Serve sprinkled with the remaining sultanas and their syrup, a little cinnamon and the toasted sesame seeds.

**SERVES 8, GENEROUSLY**

**TONY'S TIP**
You can also make this with butternut squash. Just use the same quantity and make sure you steam it until it is really tender.

In Algeria we call this Kelb el Louz, while in Egypt and Lebanon it's called Basbousa. it's very cheap to make as the main ingredient is semolina. This recipe is moist with a refreshing flavour of orange blossom.

# SEMOLINA, ALMOND & ORANGE BLOSSOM HONEY CAKE KELB EL LOUZ

50g butter or ghee, plus extra to grease
500g semolina
315g granulated sugar
50ml orange blossom water
50ml water
2 tbsp cocoa powder
75g blanched almonds

FOR THE SYRUP
250g granulated sugar
500ml water
25g honey
zest of 1 orange, cut into long, thin strands (use the large hole of a canele knife)
juice of 1 lemon
50ml orange blossom water

FOR THE PRALINE
25g blanched almonds
25g whole almonds
100g caster sugar
1 tbsp orange blossom water

Preheat the oven to 200°C/180°C fan/gas mark 6. Lightly grease a round 20cm cake tin about 4cm deep.

Put the butter, semolina, sugar, orange blossom water and water into a bowl and stir. Set aside for 15 minutes. Spoon a third of the mixture into the base of the tin. Sprinkle the cocoa powder evenly over the top. Spoon over the remaining mixture, level the surface and sprinkle over the blanched almonds.

Bake for 90 minutes until dark golden on top.

Next make the syrup. Pour the sugar into a large saucepan and add the water and honey. Bring to a simmer and cook for 5 minutes, stirring, until the sugar dissolves. Add the zest strands to the syrup with the lemon juice and orange blossom water, and simmer for 10 minutes until it has thickened and reduced by half.

Take the cake out of the oven and draw lines on the top about 3cm apart with a sharp knife. Turn the tin round and mark it again to create squares. If the tin has a loose bottom, put it on a baking tray.

Spoon the syrup evenly over the top, scattering the orange zest all over, too. Allow to cool for 2 hours.

Make the praline. Line a tray with baking parchment and arrange the nuts on it, quite close together. Heat the sugar and orange blossom water in a small saucepan over a low heat until the sugar dissolves and turns into a syrup. Increase the heat slightly and cook the syrup until it's golden to dark brown. Don't let it burn or the praline will taste bitter. Pour over the nuts and leave to set.

Chop the praline into small pieces and scatter over the cake. Use a sharp knife to slice, then serve, making sure everyone has a piece of praline and some orange zest.

**SERVES 16–18**

**DESSERTS & DRINKS**

I know that there's a tradition in the UK of using cream in pastries, and it's no different in Lebanese cuisine. This recipe looks impressive, but actually you don't need any pastry skills as it's made, very handily, from filo pastry. Once baked, douse in syrup and top with pistachio nuts.

# CRISP FILO PARCELS WITH CREAM & ROSE WATER MOUTABAG ASHTA

**FOR THE PASTRIES**
600ml double cream
75g cornflour
100ml water
5g gum mastic
220g filo pastry sheets
250g butter, melted

**FOR THE SYRUP**
250g granulated sugar
500ml water
50ml rose water
pared rind of 1 lemon

**TO SERVE**
25g finely chopped
    pistachio nuts
rose petals

Put the cream into a pan and slowly bring to the boil. Mix the cornflour with the water and pour into the pan with the gum mastic. The mixture should thicken immediately; take the pan off the heat and use a balloon whisk to mix until very smooth. Allow to cool.

Preheat the oven to 200°C/180°C fan/gas mark 6.

Unroll the filo pastry and split it into two piles of six sheets each. Put one pile to one side and cover with a clean, damp tea towel. Take the other pile of sheets and put them on a board with the long edges nearest to you. Cut them through the middle to make two long rectangles, then cut each length into six squares. You can trim the edges to make them perfect, if you want to.

Working quickly, take one square of six sheets and brush melted butter between the pieces of filo. Take one of these squares and spoon three tablespoons of the cream mixture into the middle and spread it out slightly. Fold in the points of the four corners to make a parcel. Do the same with the other five squares to make six parcels. Then make another six parcels with the covered, uncut pile of sheets, cutting and filling them in the same way.

Lift the parcels onto a baking sheet and brush with melted butter. Bake for about 20 minutes until golden.

Meanwhile, put all the syrup ingredients into a pan and bring to the boil. Simmer for 10 minutes until thickened slightly, then cool. Once cool, spoon most of the syrup over the pastry parcels.

To serve, put a parcel on each plate, spoon over a little more syrup, then sprinkle with pistachios and rose petals.

**MAKES 12**

A bit of work goes into the making of these, but they're definitely worth it. They are *sooo* delicious when freshly made and still warm. First you make a soft dough similar to choux pastry, then push it through a piping bag and nozzle to make finger-length pieces. They are then deep-fried in hot oil. A sweet syrup spooned over the top keeps the insides beautifully moist. You can keep them for a few days as the syrup preserves them but, for me, they're best when warm. They're great with mint tea, and I eat them a lot during Ramadan, after the meal to celebrate the end of the daily fast.

# ZALLABIA

200ml water
50ml milk
50g butter, chopped
150g plain flour
50g cornflour
2 large eggs, beaten
1 tsp vanilla extract
1 litre vegetable oil, for deep frying
25g pistachio nuts, finely chopped, to sprinkle

FOR THE SYRUP
500ml water
1kg caster sugar
1 piece pared lemon zest
3 tbsp orange blossom water

First make the syrup. Pour the water into a large saucepan and add the sugar and lemon zest. Heat gently to dissolve the sugar. Bring to the boil and simmer for 10 minutes. Pour into a large, flat dish and allow to cool, then stir in the orange blossom water. Set aside.

Pour the water and milk into a medium saucepan, add the butter and slowly bring to the boil, allowing the butter to melt. As soon as the water boils, add the flour and cornflour, and beat well to make a rough dough. Take the pan off the heat and whisk the mixture with an electric hand whisk until it is smooth and has cooled down, so that it is warm, rather than hot.

Slowly add the egg, a little at a time, and continue to whisk until the mixture looks and feels softer. Whisk in the vanilla extract.

Spoon the dough into a piping bag fitted with a 1.5cm star nozzle. Pipe fingers of the dough, about 4–5cm long, on to baking parchment, snipping it with scissors. (Once you become confident in doing this, you will be able to pipe and snip it straight into the hot oil.)

Heat the oil in a deep frying pan until it reaches about 190°C, or until a cube of bread browns in 20–30 seconds. Carefully lower the fingers into the hot oil and cook, in batches, until they are a golden colour – too pale and they won't be cooked inside and could fall apart in the syrup. Drain the fingers on kitchen paper.

Spoon the fried zallabia into the syrup and toss to coat. Lift them out, arrange on a platter, sprinkle with the chopped pistachios and serve.

**MAKES … PLENTY!**

The inspiration for this came from a French pastry tart filled with frangipane and fruit. I gave it my own Middle Eastern twist by adding pistachios to the frangipane mixture, then nudging sweet, ripe figs and slices of salty, chewy textured halloumi into it. It's a mixed marriage, but it really works. (See photo on page 225.)

# FIG, HALLOUMI & PISTACHIO TART

**FOR THE PASTRY**
220g plain flour, plus extra for dusting
110g room temperature butter, chopped
a pinch of salt
1 medium egg yolk
2–3 tbsp cold water

**FOR THE FRANGIPANE FILLING**
140g pistachio nuts
110g softened butter
110g golden caster sugar
1 tsp rose water
1 medium egg, beaten
20g self-raising flour
150g halloumi, thinly sliced
8 figs (about 120g), sliced

**TO SERVE**
2 generous tbsp runny honey
1–2 tsp rose water
chopped and slivered pistachio nuts
edible rose petals

You'll need a 20cm round, fluted tart tin and some baking beans.

First make the pastry. Tip the flour into a food processor and add the butter and salt. Whizz the ingredients together until the mixture resembles fine breadcrumbs.

In a small bowl, beat together the egg yolk and 2 tablespoons of cold water. Drizzle this mixture over the top of the flour mixture and pulse the mixture until it just comes together. If it looks a little dry, pour over another tablespoon of water and pulse again.

Tip the mixture into a bowl and lightly knead together. Shape into a rough, flat round, wrap in cling film and transfer to the freezer for 5 minutes.

Take the pastry out of the freezer and roll out on a lightly floured board until it's just a little larger than the tin size, so you have enough pastry to line the sides, too. Save the cling film to cover the tart once you've rolled it out. Carefully lift up the pastry and put it into the tart tin. Push the pastry into the sides of the tin, then trim any hanging over the sides. Prick all over the base with a fork, cover with the cling film you saved and transfer to the freezer again for 10–15 minutes. While the tart is chilling, preheat the oven to 200°C/180°C fan/gas mark 6.

Take the cling film off the tart, cover with baking parchment and fill the base with baking beans. Bake in the oven for 15 minutes. Carefully lift the paper and beans out of the tin and put to one side to cool. Put the tart back in the oven and bake for a further 5 minutes to dry out the pastry. Take out of the oven and allow to cool.

Turn down the oven to 180°C/160°C fan/gas mark 4.

To make the frangipane, whizz the pistachio nuts in a food processor until finely ground. Put the butter, sugar and rose water into a bowl and beat with an electric hand whisk until they look light and fluffy. Gradually add the beaten egg, whisking well to make sure it mixes evenly into the butter mixture.

Add the flour and ground pistachio nuts to the bowl and fold the mixture together to make a paste.

Once the pastry has cooled, spread the frangipane over the base, right up to the edges. Position the tart case in front of you and lay slices of figs in a round in the frangipane. Follow that with a row of halloumi and repeat until you reach the bottom of the tart.

Bake in the oven for 40 minutes until golden. Mix together the honey and rose water, and brush all over the top. Scatter over the pistachios and rose petals. Leave to cool in the tin until warm, then carefully remove the tart and transfer to a serving plate or board.

Slice into pieces and serve.

**SERVES 12**

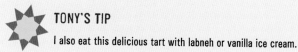

### TONY'S TIP

I also eat this delicious tart with labneh or vanilla ice cream.

This is a recipe straight from the heart of my home. When I was a little boy, whenever my mother made these little sweet walnut cigars, I would sneak into the kitchen and steal some, freshly made, from the plate. One time, I ate the entire batch. My mother was so embarrassed that she didn't have any to serve to our guests. Even now, she reminds me of how I used to embarrass her! And, of course, I still love eating them just as much today.

# WALNUT & CINNAMON HONEY CIGARS

FOR THE CIGARS
**300g walnut halves**
**135g caster sugar**
**1 tsp cinnamon**
**generous pinch of grated nutmeg**
**50g butter, melted**
**5 tbsp orange blossom water**
**10 sheets feuille de brick pastry**
**1 medium egg, beaten**
**vegetable or sunflower oil, for frying**

FOR THE SYRUP
**150g runny honey**
**2 tbsp orange blossom water**

TO SERVE
**1 tbsp sesame seeds**
**a few rose petals**

Preheat the oven to 200°C/180°C fan/gas mark 6. Put the walnuts on a baking sheet and roast them for 6 minutes until they're just golden and have that lovely nutty, fragrant aroma.

Set 50g aside and put the rest into a small food processor. Whizz until they have broken down into a grainy powder. Take care not to overwork them or they'll become oily and too paste-like for this recipe.

Tip into a bowl and add the sugar, spices, butter and orange blossom water. Mix together to form a paste – it'll feel a bit like marzipan.

Trim a sheet of the pastry to make a 20cm square. Cut the square in half to make two long rectangles, with the short sides nearest you.

Use a teaspoon to scoop up some of the nut mixture – squeeze it down on the spoon into an oval shape. Lay it at the bottom of one of the rectangles, about 1cm from the bottom, and roll up the pastry, tucking in the sides as you go. Brush the edges with beaten egg to seal.

Do the same with the rest of the pastry, nut mixture and egg, until you've made about 20 cigars.

Heat a couple of tablespoons of oil in a large frying pan and fry the pastry cigars until golden. Drain on a plate lined with kitchen paper.

Pour the honey and orange blossom water into a small saucepan and heat gently for 5 minutes to warm the honey. Dip each cigar into the honey, drain well, then arrange on a platter. Chop the remaining walnuts into small pieces and sprinkle over the cigars along with the sesame seeds and rose petals to serve.

**MAKES ABOUT 20**

**DESSERTS & DRINKS**

Oranges, almonds and orange blossom water are three ingredients that we always have at home. They marry together perfectly in this recipe – the nuts enhance the bitter sweet oranges while the flower water adds a fragrant touch. This is one of my favourites and it's also one of the most popular with the customers in our restaurants.

Although I've called this a cake, it's just like a pudding when it's served straight from the oven. The process of simmering the oranges until tender then puréeing them helps to give it a unique slightly soft and mousse-like texture. It's superb!

# GLUTEN-FREE ORANGE & ALMOND CAKE

butter, for greasing
3 oranges
300g caster sugar
6–7 medium eggs –
    350g in weight
250g ground almonds
zest of 1 orange – not
    too fine as it's lovely to
    bite into and taste the
    zing of the zest
2 tbsp orange blossom
    water

FOR THE TOPPING
2 large oranges, each cut
    into 5–6 slices about
    4–5mm thick
100g caster sugar
3 tbsp honey, plus a
    little extra to glaze
300ml water
2 tbsp orange blossom
    water
25g butter

TO SERVE
labneh
orange zest

Grease and line a 25cm round loose-bottomed cake tin with baking parchment.

Put the whole oranges in a small saucepan, cover with water and a lid, and bring to the boil. Turn the heat down and simmer for 1½ hours, or until the oranges are tender.

When they are cooked, preheat the oven to 170°C/150°C fan/gas mark 3.

Drain the oranges, reserving the syrup, then slice them into quarters. Remove and discard the ends of stalks and any seeds, then put the oranges into a food processor and blitz to a purée.

Tip the sugar into a large bowl and add the eggs. Whisk with an electric hand whisk for 5-10 minutes until the mixture is thick and foamy.

Add the ground almonds, orange zest, orange blossom water and orange purée, and fold in until the mixture is smooth. Pour into the cake tin.

Bake in the oven for 1-1½ hours, until golden. Push a skewer into the centre: if it comes out clean, the cake is ready. Cool in the tin for 15 minutes, then on a wire rack.

For the topping, put the orange slices into a small saucepan and add the caster sugar, 2 tablespoons of the honey, the water and the orange blossom water. Allow the sugar to dissolve, then simmer the slices until tender but still whole, about 5–8 minutes. Drain well.

Heat half the butter in a frying pan over a low heat and add half the slices. Cook for a minute or two, then drizzle over half the remaining honey until one side caramelises. Turn to cook the other side. Repeat with the rest of the slices until they are all glistening and golden.

Starting from the outer edge of the cake arrange the orange slices slightly overlapping, leaving a 2–3cm border round the edge, until you reach the middle. You'll need 11 or 12 slices to make it look really chic.

Mix an extra 2 tablespoons of honey with 2 tablespoons of the reserved syrup and brush over the top to glaze.

Spoon the labneh into a bowl, scatter with orange zest and serve alongside the cake.

**SERVES 12**

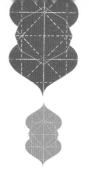

I love mixing different flavours when I'm eating and it's the same when I'm experimenting in the kitchen. With any ingredient, I like to think: What else can I make with it? I was brought up eating lots of aubergines. They were used in so many different recipes, and the finished dishes were always savoury. I had an idea for using it in a sweet tart and even before I made this I imagined how it would taste with all the ingredients working together. I got a few looks when I mentioned using aubergines in a dessert to my friends, but as soon as they tried it they loved it. If you're using Greek yoghurt, make sure you buy the traditional thick variety rather than Greek-style yoghurt, as the filling needs to be firm enough to hold the roasted aubergine. If you want to get ahead and make this even easier, prepare the pastry the day before and keep it in an airtight container in a cool place. (See photo on page 233.)

# MY ROASTED AUBERGINE, ROSE, HONEY & LABNEH TART

### FOR THE PASTRY
220g plain flour, plus a
  little extra for dusting
110g room temperature
  butter, chopped
pinch of salt
1 medium egg yolk
2–3 tbsp cold water

### FOR THE FILLING
2 medium aubergines
  (about 600g), chopped
  into 1.5–2cm cubes
3 tbsp olive oil
3 tbsp runny honey
1–2 tbsp rose water
15g butter, softened
500g labneh or thick
  Greek yoghurt (not
  Greek-style)
zest of 1 orange or
  1 lemon
2 tbsp rose syrup or
  grenadine

You need a 20cm round shallow tart tin. Start by making the pastry; this is the same pastry base as for the Fig, Halloumi & Pistachio Tart (see page 226). Tip the flour into a food processor and add the butter and salt. Whizz the ingredients together until the mixture resembles fine breadcrumbs.

In a small bowl, beat together the egg yolk and 2 tablespoons of cold water. Drizzle this over the top of the flour mixture and pulse until it just comes together. If it looks a little dry, pour over the remaining tablespoon of water and pulse again.

Tip the mixture into a bowl and lightly knead together. Shape into a rough, flat round, wrap in cling film and transfer to the freezer for 5 minutes.

Take the pastry out of the freezer and roll out on a lightly floured board until it's just a little larger than the tin size, so you have enough pastry to line the sides, too. Save the cling film to wrap over the tart once you've rolled it out. Carefully lift the pastry and put into the tart tin. Push into the corners and sides of the tin, then trim any pastry hanging over the side. Prick the base all over with a fork, cover again with the cling film and transfer to the freezer for 10–15 minutes.

25g slivered pistachio
  nuts
25g blanched almonds,
  roasted
1 tbsp toasted sesame
  seeds
petals from rose-petal
  jam

While the pastry is chilling, preheat the oven to 200°C/180°C fan/gas mark 6.

Take the cling film off the tart, cover with baking parchment and fill the base with baking beans. Bake in the oven for 15 minutes. Carefully lift the paper and beans out of the tart tin and put to one side to cool. Put the tart back in the oven and bake for a further 5 minutes to dry out the pastry. Take out of the oven and allow to cool. Once cool, take the pastry case out of the tart tin, put on a serving plate and set aside.

Put the chopped aubergines into a roasting tin and pour the oil over them. Toss together. Roast in the oven for 40–50 minutes until each piece is a rich golden brown. Mix 2 tablespoons of the honey with the rose water and drizzle over the aubergines, toss together, then dot the butter over the top. Return to the oven for another 5 minutes so the butter mixture is absorbed into the aubergines. Take the tin out of the oven and allow the aubergines to cool.

Spoon the labneh into a bowl and fold in the orange zest, the remaining tablespoon of honey and the rose syrup, to give the filling a luscious pink hue. Transfer into the pastry base and spread out. Spoon the aubergines on top, making sure the pieces are scattered evenly over the yoghurt. Sprinkle over the pistachios, blanched almonds and sesame seeds, and, finally, dot a few rose petals from the jam over the top.

**SERVES 12**

Mint tea is very popular in Arabic countries, especially Morocco. There are many ways to make it, not just by dropping a big bunch of mint into hot water – though that is delicious. I like to use white tea leaves, a drizzle of honey and a generous quantity of fresh mint leaves, then finish it with a few drops of orange blossom water. Whenever I make this I am always asked for the recipe.

If you've never tried white tea before, it's made from leaves that are picked and dried without having time to oxidise. When brewed, the taste is lighter than black or green tea, so it is perfect for this. You can also make and chill it, then serve it with lots of ice as iced tea.

# FRESH MINT & ORANGE BLOSSOM TEA SHAY BIL NAÂNAÂ

2 tbsp white tea leaves, such as Silver Tip
1.2 litres hot water
2 strips pared orange peel
bunch of mint
2 tbsp orange blossom water
honey or sugar, to taste

Boil a kettle of water. Put the tea leaves in a teapot or, if you don't have one, a large jug.

Pour the hot water over the tea leaves. Add the pared orange peel, mint and orange blossom water, and allow to brew for 2-3 minutes; the tea should be quite light in colour.

Strain through a tea strainer (or small sieve), dividing it among six small glasses, and sweeten with sugar or honey, if you like.

**SERVES 6**

The funny thing about this drink is that even though it has café in the title, it doesn't contain any coffee. Instead, it's a delicate balance of ingredients – rose water, orange blossom or both – mixed with hot water that is a lovely refreshing way to end a meal. I like to serve it with a cardamom pod in each cup so it doesn't look like just a cup of hot water. It's the perfect drink if you're feeling a little bit too full after a big meal.

# CAFÉ BLANC

600ml water
3 tbsp honey
5 tbsp orange blossom
   water
3 cardamom pods,
   crushed, plus extra
   pods to serve
Deglet Noor dates and
   whole almonds,
   to serve

Pour the water into a saucepan and bring to the boil. Take off the heat and add the honey, orange blossom water and crushed cardamom pods. Stir everything together, then strain into six small cups and drop a cardamom pod into each cup before serving. Put a couple of dates and almonds on the side to serve.

**SERVES 6**

If you've never had this, let me describe it to you – it looks like hot milk, but has a moreish silky texture and a fragrant flavour enhanced by an extra dash of flower water. It's normally drunk in the winter as it's so warming, but I drink it all year round, especially when there's a kaak stick on offer. Dipping these slightly sweet breadsticks (flavoured with sesame and fennel seeds) into it reminds me of breakfast as a little boy, dunking my cakes or biscuits in milky coffee. Every time I have sahlab and kaak sticks, it makes me feel like I'm a kid again.

# SAHLAB

1 litre milk
1 cinnamon stick
250g sahlab orchid
    powder
2 tbsp orange blossom
    water
2 tbsp rose water

TO SERVE
cinnamon, for sprinkling
kaak sticks (see below)

Pour the milk into a saucepan and add the cinnamon stick. Heat gently to bring slowly to the boil, then gradually pour in the sahlab powder, stirring continuously. Simmer, stirring, until the powder has dissolved.

Lift the pan off the heat and stir in the orange blossom and rose water. Divide among six cups and sprinkle a little cinnamon over each. Serve with kaak sticks.

**SERVES 6**

### TONY'S TIP

You can buy kaak sticks but they're nicer if homemade, and they keep in an airtight container for up to 5 days. Sift 250g bread flour into a bowl. Add ½ tablespoon yeast, 1 teaspoon salt and 1 tablespoon caster sugar. Make a well in the middle and pour in 50ml water, 50ml milk and 60ml vegetable oil. Stir together, adding more water if needed. Knead to make a soft dough. Put in a clean bowl, cover, then leave to rise for 1 hour. Roll a small ball of dough into a thin 12cm strip on a lightly oiled board. Repeat to use all the dough. Put on a baking sheet to prove for 20 minutes. Preheat the oven to 200°C/180°C fan/gas mark 6. Brush with beaten egg, then sprinkle over black and white sesame and fennel seeds. Bake for 10 minutes, then lower the oven to 140°C/120°C fan/gas mark 1 and bake until golden and cooked through. Cool before serving.

One of my weaknesses is that I love anything sweet. I would, if I could, tuck into all the delightful Middle Eastern pastries there are. Chocolate is also a favourite, and mixed with halva the two work magically together, each enhancing the flavour of the other.

This drink is very rich and is laced with a little tahina to give it a lovely silky texture. It's the sort of thing I might make at a weekend when I'm cooking brunch for friends. And I make it for my nephews, who love it. They sometimes pop in on a Sunday morning on the pretence that they've come to see me, when in fact all they want is for me to rustle up a couple of mugs of this! I always oblige, of course ...

# COMPTOIR SPICED HOT CHOCOLATE WITH TAHINA & HALVA

50g dark chocolate (about 60% cocoa solids), grated
30g tahina
½–1 tsp cinnamon, plus extra to serve
15g halva, crumbled
400ml milk, or use coconut milk, if you prefer
honey or sugar to sweeten – 1 tbsp is plenty for two

TO SERVE
crumbled halva – be generous with it
chopped or slivered pistachio nuts

In a large bowl, mix the grated chocolate, tahina, cinnamon and halva.

Pour the milk into a saucepan and bring to the boil. As soon as it boils, pour on to the chocolate mixture and whisk well.

Pour the mixture back into the pan and heat gently, whisking continuously until the chocolate has completely melted. If you have a coffee frother, you can use it to make the mixture extra frothy.

Divide between two glasses, sprinkle over the crumbled halva, pistachios and an extra pinch of cinnamon, and serve.

**SERVES 6**

DESSERTS & DRINKS

All the ingredients that go into this drink can be found in a typical Middle Eastern kitchen – dates (especially the Deglet Noor variety), roasted almonds, creamy labneh and orange blossom water (see photo on page 241). This smoothie can be made as healthy – or as indulgent and rich-tasting – as you like. I often drink it to break the fast during Ramadan, but I also drink it in the mornings. If you've never tried orange blossom water, start with one tablespoon and add more until you have the desired flavour. For a lighter smoothie, swap the labneh for Greek or low-fat natural yoghurt. It will thicken over time so drink it soon after making.

# DATE, ALMOND, ORANGE BLOSSOM & LABNEH SMOOTHIE
## MASHROOB HADJ CHABANE

100g roasted, blanched almonds, roughly chopped
24 Deglet Noor or 15 Medjool dates, depending on what's available
250g labneh
500ml milk
3–4 tbsp orange blossom water
runny honey, to taste

Put the nuts into the bowl of a food processor and blitz to make a fine powder. Don't overwork them or they'll turn oily. Next, add the dates and blend them well with the nuts. They need to be blitzed to a purée otherwise they will fall to the bottom of the glass when you serve this.

Add the labneh and blend again, then add the add the milk slowly with the motor still running, and continue to blend until the mixture is smooth. Blend in the orange blossom water next, and sweeten with honey to taste.

Divide among six glasses and serve.

**SERVES 6**

Every time I take a bite of watermelon it brings back a distinct memory of my father walking into the kitchen holding a huge watermelon. All the family would sit in the courtyard overlooking the garden – Mum, Grandma, aunts, uncles and cousins – and take freshly cut chunks dripping with sweet juice from the middle of the table. (See photo on page 242.)

# WATERMELON LEMONADE

1 medium watermelon,
  skinned – about 2.5kg
  flesh
150ml lemon juice –
  about 5 juicy lemons
4–6 tbsp orange blossom
  water
4 tbsp runny honey, or
  to taste
pumpkin seeds, to serve

Trim any white bits from the skinned melon with a sharp knife and pick out all the black seeds and throw them away.

Roughly chop the flesh and put in a food processor or blender. Whizz to crush the flesh into a juice. Stir in the lemon juice, orange blossom water and honey to taste. The amount of honey you need will depend on the ripeness of the watermelon.

There should be a good balance of sweet, sharp and scented as a result of the orange blossom water. Serve with the pumpkin seeds scattered on top.

**SERVES 6–8**

We always have mint and lemons at home so this is a really easy drink to put together. Just a handful of ingredients go into this summer cooler, but, boy, does it pack a punch. It's a little bit sweet, a little bit sour – all mixed together with refreshing mint. (See photo on page 241.)

# FROZEN MINT LEMONADE

100g mint
juice of 4 large, ripe
  lemons
juice of 4 large, ripe
  limes
3 tbsp orange blossom or
  rose water
caster sugar or honey,
  to taste
crushed ice, to serve

Blend the mint with a little water in a food processor or blender until it is reduced down to a juice.

Add the lemon juice, lime juice and orange blossom or rose water, and blend again, then add sugar or honey to sweeten, to your taste.

Pour into a large bowl and add about six glasses of crushed ice. Stir everything together and divide among six glasses to serve.

**SERVES 6**

This version of lemonade is served in every Tunisian home in summer. The first time I had it was at the home of my friend Ines, her husband Amir and their family. It tasted just like lemon tart in a glass and was so different that I couldn't get enough of it. The reason it's so unusual is that you simmer lemons until they are tender, then add sugar and vanilla. The softened fruit is blitzed with the syrup to make a purée. When you blend it, the mixture has to be thickish, so that it has a good texture when mixed with the ice and water. (See photo on page 242.)

# VANILLA CITRONNADE

7 unwaxed lemons,
  halved, pips removed
1 litre cold water
1½ vanilla pods
500g caster sugar

TO SERVE
ice cubes
still water
20–30 whole blanched
  almonds

Put the lemon halves in a saucepan and add the water and vanilla pods. Cover the pan with a lid and bring to the boil. As soon as it's boiling, turn the heat down low so the water is just simmering – you don't want too much of the water to evaporate as it's going to be simmering for a while.

Simmer for about 1 hour, until the lemons start to soften and feel tender enough to mash – check them with the point of a sharp knife. Add the sugar, stir it in, and bring gently back to the boil. Simmer for another hour or so, until the lemons are very soft.

Lift the lemons out of the liquid and put in a bowl to cool. At this stage you might find more pips; if so remove and discard them now. Set the pan to one side as you need the syrup to blend with the lemons.

Once the lemons and syrup are cool, put the lemons in a blender and whizz to make a purée. Pour about 600ml syrup into the blender. Split the vanilla pods by running a sharp knife down the middle of each and remove the seeds. Add these to the blender, too. Blitz until smooth.

Taste the mixture and check it's sweet enough. If you prefer it sweeter, add more syrup and blend again.

If you have a crowd round, you can make this up in a jug. Just add ice and about 1 litre still water. Stir well so the base is thoroughly mixed with the water. Pour into glasses and top each with two or three blanched almonds.

**SERVES 10**

### TONY'S TIP

If you don't drink this straight away, it will keep in the fridge for up to a week, or freeze it in ice cube trays for up to a month

We always had lots of oranges and lemons at home when I was a kid because my father would buy crates of them from the farmers in the market. This drink reminds me of those times. I soak oranges and lemons with crushed ice, a little sugar, some orange blossom water and rose water. You might think the process unusual, but the end result is utterly delicious. After the fruit has been soaked and the ice has melted, the juice and bitter flavour of the skin of the fruit is squeezed out to create the drink, and it's this bitterness that adds a real kick. The flavour is a cross between Turkish delight and bitter lemons, and it makes a fantastic cooler on a hot summer's day (see photo on page 241). Sahtein!

# LEBANESE LEMONADE

11 large oranges
5 lemons
2 tbsp caster sugar, or to taste
6 tbsp orange blossom water
6 tbsp rose water
4 big cups of crushed ice, plus extra ice cubes to serve

leaves from a few sprigs of mint, to serve

Chop ten of the oranges and four of the lemons by halving them, then cutting each half into quarters. Put in a large bowl. Add the caster sugar, orange blossom water, rose water and crushed ice. Set aside for several hours or cover the bowl and leave it in a cool place overnight.

Once the fruit has soaked for a few hours and all the ice has melted, take each piece of fruit and crush it with your hands. Squeeze hard so the juice runs into the bowl and retains the bitter flavour of the skin.

Strain into a large, clean jug. Zest about half the remaining orange and lemon, and stir the zest into the juice. Slice the rest and add to the jug. Finely chop half the mint leaves and add to the jug, too. Add a couple of handfuls of ice and float a few of the remaining mint leaves on top.

Divide the lemonade evenly among six–eight glasses, making sure that a few bits of ice, fruit and mint drop into each one, and serve.

**SERVES 6-8**

 **TONY'S TIP**
Don't hold back on the orange blossom water, as this brings the flavour of the fresh orange to life. When I make this, I taste it before serving, then usually add a splash or two more to balance it.

FEAST MENUS

Feasts are all about sharing good food with friends and family; food that you can't wait to eat and – usually in my culture – lots of it. The feast might be to mark an occasion or celebration, or just be cooked because it's Sunday morning. It doesn't matter whether the feast is for two, ten or twenty guests, the table will always be full. At the end of the meal nothing is wasted. Any food left over becomes a gift for the guest to take home and share with their family. This is a very important part of our culture.

Traditionally all our Middle Eastern feasts are served with a selection of breads (Arabic breads, flatbreads, freshly-baked homemade breads, and so on) and always with lots of fresh mint and orange blossom tea, so please assume that these go with every meal. However, this is your feast, so use these menus as a guide for interesting flavour pairings and ideas. There really is no right or wrong, the only rule is, if you fancy it, you should definitely try it!

## WEEKEND FEAST

This is a rather special selection of dishes that together make a perfect weekend feast. It needs a little preparation, so it's one for when you have time to keep an eye on recipes and can enjoy the cooking as much as the event.

Hommos with Lamb & Pine Nuts (page 57)
Labneh Dip (page 58)
Spiced Potatoes (page 71)
Spiced Lamb Pastries (page 78)
Feta & Nigella Seed Falafel (page 82)
Palestinian Braised Spiced Chicken Pie (page 130)
Green Lentil & Rice Salad (page 186)
Stuffed Cabbage Leaves with Spiced Minced Lamb &
  Rice (page 200)
Pomegranate & Pistachio Cheesecake (page 212)
Lebanese Lemonade (page 245)

## BRUNCH FEAST

A long, lazy brunch with friends can be just the thing at the weekend. This mixture of recipes combines savoury and sweet, hot and cold. There is plenty to share and fill you up to start the day.

Feta with Olive Oil & Za'atar (page 25)
Aubergine Shakshuka (page 18)
Sujuk Scrambled Eggs (page 26)
Lebanese Village Breakfast (page 32)
Pastries Stuffed with Feta and Halloumi (page 80)
Labneh & Caramelised Banana Wrap (page 38)
Fresh Mint & Orange Blossom Tea (page 236)
Comptoir Spiced Hot Chocolate with Tahina & Halva (page 239)

## MY BIG FAT FEAST FROM THE MIDDLE EAST

As I've already said, if I cook for family and friends you won't be able to see the table for all the wonderful food on it. With so many fabulous dishes, this menu is perfect for any big occasion or holiday, and the slow-cooked lamb is the most incredible showstopper.

Beetroot Hommos and Hommos with Lamb & Pine Nuts (page 57)
Broad Bean & Tahina Dip (page 66)
Labneh Dip (page 58)
Aleppo Roast Peppers & Mixed Nut Dip (page 70)
Chicken Livers with Cherry Tomatoes & Pomegranate Molasses
  (page 76)
Feta & Nigella Seed Falafel (page 82)
Pastries Stuffed with Feta & Halloumi (page 80)
Pumpkin & Saffron Soup (page 160)
Slow-cooked Shoulder of Lamb (page 124)
My Mum Zohra's Fried Sardines (page 146)
Chicken & Chickpea Stew (page 176)
Tahina, Chocolate & Pistachio Cheesecake (page 213)
Crisp Filo Parcels with Cream & Rose Water (page 220)
Walnut & Cinnamon Honey Cigars (page 228)
Vanilla Citronnade (page 244)

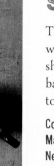

## SUMMER FEAST

This is a great feast for summer, as it uses all the wonderful vegetables that are in season. If the sun is shining all the meat and fish can be cooked on the barbecue - cooking over coals adds another dimension to the flavours.

Courgette & Tahina Dip (page 63)
Marinated Chicken Wings (page 72)
New Potatoes & Green Tahina Salad (page 98)
Village Tomato Salad (page 100)
Aubergine & Spiced Minced-Lamb Kebabs (page 136)
Monkfish & Roasted Pepper Kebabs (page 153)
Stuffed Courgettes in a Yoghurt Sauce (page 172)
Grilled Chopped Aubergine Salad (page 90)
Roasted Pepper Salad (page 94)
Rose Mouhalabia with Summer Fruit Compote (page 214)
Zallabia (page 222)
Frozen Mint Lemonade (page 243)
Watermelon Lemonade (page 243)

## THE QUICK FEAST

We all find ourselves short of time sometimes, but that doesn't mean that we should sacrifice the quality of the food we eat. This simple feast can be put together really quickly as there is little cooking or preparation required for any of the recipes.

Labneh Dip (page 58)
Butter Bean Salad (page 96)
Roasted Chicken & Couscous Salad (page 86)
Bulgar Wheat & Tomato Salad (page 198)
Cauliflower & Tahina (page 119)
Fresh Mint & Orange Blossom Tea (page 236)

# VEGETARIAN FEAST

This is a wonderful menu for a feast in which
beautiful vegetables take centre stage – whether you
are vegetarian, are cooking for vegetarians or just want
to reduce your meat consumption without losing any
of the flavours you love.

Broad Bean & Tahina Dip (page 66)
Artichoke Heart & Tahina Dip (page 67)
Spiced Potatoes (page 71)
Fried Vegetables with Yoghurt & Tahina Sauce (page 68)
Grilled Chopped Aubergine Salad (page 90)
Roasted Pepper Salad (page 94)
Stuffed Swiss Chard with Spiced Rice & Vegetables (page 194)
Gluten-free Orange & Almond Cake (page 230)
Lebanese Lemonade (page 245)

# INDEX

Page numbers in *italic* refer to the photographs

## A

Aleppo Roast Peppers & Mixed Nut Dip 70
allspice 11
almonds: Date, Almond, Orange Blossom & Labneh Smoothie 240-1, *242*
Gluten-free Orange & Almond Cake 230-1, *231*
Semolina, Almond & Orange Blossom Honey Cake 218, *219*
Arabic Bread 51
*Arnabit bil Tarator* 119
Artichoke Heart & Tahina Dip 65, *67*
artichokes *see* globe artichokes
aubergines: Aubergine & Halloumi Omelette 20, *21*
Aubergine & Pomegranate Salad *92*, *93*
Aubergine & Spiced Minced-Lamb Kebabs 136-7, *137*
Aubergine & Walnut Dip *61*, 62
Aubergine Shakshuka 18, *19*
Baby Aubergines with Spiced Minced Lamb & Tahina 168-9, *170-1*
Bulgar Wheat with Chicken 188, *189*
Grilled Chopped Aubergine Salad 90, *91*
My Roasted Aubergine, Rose, Honey & Labneh Tart *233*, 234-5
Palestinian Spiced Rice with Chicken 184, *185*
Spiced Potatoes 71
Syrian Aubergine Salad 118

## B

*Baba bil Joz* 61, 62
*Bamia bil Zeyt* 116, *117*
bananas: Labneh & Caramelised Banana Wrap 38, *39*
*Batata Harra* 71
*Batata Helwa bil Tahina* 216, *217*
*Batenjan wa Halloumi* 20, *21*

beetroot: Beetroot, Fig & Feta Salad 104, *105*
Beetroot Hommos *54-5*, 57
*Beyd bil Sujuk* 26, *27*
black peppercorns 11
bread: Arabic Bread 51
Date Brioche *43*, 44-5
Feta & Spinach Flatbreads *46-7*, 49
Fig & Feta Tartine 28, *29*
Fried Red Mullet with Crisp Bread & Tahina 144, *145*
Labneh & Caramelised Banana Wrap 38, *39*
Lebanese Village Breakfast 30-1, 33
Palestinian Braised Spiced Chicken Pie 130, *131*
Sesame Seed Bread 50
Spiced Tomato Flatbreads *46-7*, 48
Bream with Tahina Sauce 140, *141*
Brioche, Date *43*, 44-5
broad beans: Braised Broad Beans with Olive Oil 108, *109*
Broad Bean & Tahina Dip 65, 66
Broad Beans in a Tomato Sauce 34, *35*
Ful Salad with Radish & Mint 112, *113*
Lamb & Artichoke Stew 164, *165*
Brunch feast 246
bulgar wheat 10
Bulgar Wheat & Spiced Minced Lamb Pie 190-1, *191*
Bulgar Wheat & Tomato Salad 198, *199*
Bulgar Wheat with Chicken 188, *189*
Potato & Spiced Minced Lamb Pie 178-9, *179*
*see also* cracked wheat
*Burghul bil Dajaj* 188, *189*
Butter Bean Salad 96, *97*
butternut squash: Roasted Chicken & Couscous Salad 86-7, *87*

## C

cabbage: Stuffed Cabbage Leaves with Spiced Minced Lamb & Rice 200, *201*

Café Blanc 237
cakes: Gluten-free Orange & Almond Cake 230-1, *231*
Semolina, Almond & Orange Blossom Honey Cake 218, *219*
caramel: Caramelised Bananas 38, *39*
Caramelised Poached Quinces 40, *41*
Praline 218
caraway 11
cardamom pods 11
Café Blanc 237
carrots: Chicken & Chickpea Stew 176, *177*
Lamb & Artichoke Stew 164, *165*
cauliflower: Cauliflower & Tahina 119
cheese: Aubergine & Halloumi Omelette 20, *21*
Aubergine Shakshuka 18, *19*
Beetroot, Fig & Feta Salad 104, *105*
Feta & Nigella Seed Falafel 82, *83*
Feta & Spinach Flatbreads *46-7*, 49
Feta with Olive Oil & Za'atar *22-3*, 25
Feta with Pistachios & Date Syrup *22-3*, 25
Feta with Sesame Seeds & Honey *22-3*, 25
Feta with Tomatoes & Spring Onions *22-3*, 24
Fig & Feta Tartine 28, *29*
Fig, Halloumi & Pistachio Tart *224-5*, *226-7*
Grilled Halloumi with Roasted Vine Tomatoes 102, *103*
Lebanese Village Breakfast 30-1, 33
Pastries Stuffed with Feta & Halloumi 80, *81*
Roasted Pepper & Feta Salad *113*, 114, *115*
Shredded Filo & Cheese Pudding with a Rose-Honey Syrup 208, *209*
Za'atar-crusted Halloumi 84, *85*
cheesecake: Pomegranate Pistachio Cheesecake 210-11, *213*
Tahina, Chocolate & Pistachio Cheesecake *210-11*, 212

chicken: Baby Chicken with Lemon
    Juice & Potatoes 128, *129*
  Bulgar Wheat with Chicken 188,
    *189*
  Chicken & Chickpea Stew 176,
    *177*
  Freekeh with Chicken 196, *197*
  Giant Couscous with Chicken
    *202-3*, 204-5
  Lebanese Chicken Soup 162, *163*
  Marinated Chicken Wings 72, *73*
  Palestinian Braised Spiced
    Chicken Pie 130, *131*
  Palestinian Spiced Rice with
    Chicken 184, *185*
  Roasted Chicken & Couscous
    Salad 86-7, *87*
  Spiced Roast Chicken 126, *127*
  Chicken Livers with Cherry
    Tomatoes & Pomegranate
    Molasses 76, *77*
chickpeas 12
  Beetroot Hommos *54-5*, 57
  Bulgar Wheat with Chicken 188,
    *189*
  Chicken & Chickpea Stew 176,
    *177*
  Chickpeas with Yoghurt &
    Tahina Sauce 174, *175*
  Classic Hommos *54-5*, 56
  Feta & Nigella Seed Falafel 82, *83*
  Ful Salad with Radish & Mint
    112, *113*
  Giant Couscous with Chicken
    *202-3*, 204-5
  Hommos Beiruty *54-5*, 57
  Hommos with Lamb & Pine Nuts
    *54-5*, 57
  Red Pepper Hommos *54-5*, 57
chilli flakes and chilli powder 12
chillies: Aleppo Roast Peppers &
    Mixed Nut Dip 70
  Feta & Nigella Seed Falafel 82, *83*
  Harissa Sauce 74, *75*
  Roasted Pepper Salad 94, *95*
  Spiced Roast Chicken 126, *127*
chocolate: Comptoir Spiced Hot
    Chocolate with Tahina &
    Halva 239
  Tahina, Chocolate & Pistachio
    Cheesecake *210-11*, 212
cider vinegar 12
Cigars, Walnut & Cinnamon Honey
    228, *229*
cinnamon 12

Citronnade, Vanilla 244
Comptoir Spiced Hot Chocolate
  with Tahina & Halva 239
coriander: Cuttlefish with Garlic,
  Lemon & Coriander 148, *149*
coriander (spice) 12
courgettes: Courgette & Tahina Dip
  *61*, 63
  Scrambled Eggs with Lamb &
    Courgettes 36, *37*
  Stuffed Courgettes in a Yoghurt
    Sauce 172, *173*
couscous 12
  Giant Couscous with Chicken
    *202-3*, 204-5
  Roasted Chicken & Couscous
    Salad 86-7, *87*
cracked wheat: Tabbouleh 144, *145*
  *see also* bulgar wheat
cream: Crisp Filo Parcels with
  Cream & Rose Water 220, *221*
  Rose Mouhalabiah with Summer
    Fruit Compote 214, *215*
  Sweet Potato & Tahina Pudding
    216, *217*
cream cheese: Pomegranate &
  Pistachio Cheesecake *210-11*,
    213
  Tahina, Chocolate & Pistachio
    Cheesecake *210-11*, 212
cucumber: Cucumber & Yoghurt
  Sauce 191
  Freekeh with Chicken 196, *197*
cumin 13
Cuttlefish with Garlic, Lemon &
  Coriander 148, *149*

**D**

*Dajaj Mashwi* 126, *127*
dates: Date, Almond, Orange
  Blossom & Labneh Smoothie
    *240-1*, 242
  Date Brioche *43*, 44-5
  Feta with Pistachios & Date
    Syrup *22-3*, 25
dips: Artichoke Heart & Tahina
    65, 67
  Aubergine & Walnut *61*, 62
  Broad Bean & Tahina 65, 66
  Courgette & Tahina *61*, 63
  Hommos *54-5*, 56-7
  Labneh 58, *59*
dried fruit 13
  Labneh with Caramelised

Poached Quinces & Spiced
  Dried Fruit 40, *41*
Slow-Cooked Shoulder of Lamb
  *122-3*, 124-5
drinks: Café Blanc 237
  Comptoir Spiced Hot Chocolate
    with Tahina & Halva 239
  Date, Almond, Orange Blossom &
    Labneh Smoothie *240-1*, 242
  Fresh Mint & Orange Blossom
    Tea 236
  Frozen Mint Lemonade *240-1*,
    243
  Lebanese Lemonade 245
  Sahlab 238
  Vanilla Citronnade 244
  Watermelon Lemonade *240-1*,
    243

**E**

eggs: Aubergine & Halloumi
    Omelette 20, *21*
  Aubergine Shakshuka 18, *19*
  Lebanese Village Breakfast *30-1*,
    33
  Scrambled Eggs with Lamb &
    Courgettes 36, *37*
  Sujuk Scrambled Eggs 26, *27*

**F**

falafel: Feta & Nigella Seed Falafel
    82, *83*
  Lebanese Village Breakfast *30-1*,
    32
*Fattet Makdous* 168-9, *170-1*
fava beans 13
  Broad Beans in a Tomato Sauce
    34, *35*
fennel: Monkfish & Roasted Pepper
    Kebab 153
  Sautéed Prawns with Spiced
    Braised Fennel 152
feta cheese *see* cheese
figs: Beetroot, Fig & Feta Salad 104,
    *105*
  Fig & Feta Tartine 28, *29*
  Fig, Halloumi & Pistachio Tart
    *224-5*, 226-7
filo pastry: Crisp Filo Parcels 220,
    *221*
  Shredded Filo & Cheese Pudding
    208, *209*
fish *see* sardines, sea bass *etc*

flatbreads: Feta & Spinach
Flatbreads *46-7*, 49
Labneh & Caramelised Banana
Wrap 38, *39*
Spiced Tomato Flatbreads *46-7*,
48
*Fool Akdar bil Zeyt* 108, *109*
*Foolyah 65, 66*
*Fotoor Araby 30-1, 33*
frangipane: Fig, Halloumi &
Pistachio Tart *224-5, 226-7*
freekeh 13
Freekeh with Chicken 196, *197*
*Frekeh bil Dajaj* 196, *197*
French Beans in a Tomato & Olive
Oil Sauce 106, *107*
Frozen Mint Lemonade *240-1*, 243
fruit: Rose Mouhalabiah with
Summer Fruit Compote 214, *215*
ful beans 13
*Ful Medames* 34, *35*
Ful Salad with Radish & Mint
112, *113*

## G

garlic: My Mum Zohra's Fried
Sardines *146-7, 147*
Giant Couscous with Chicken
*202-3, 204-5*
globe artichokes: Artichoke &
Tahina Soup *156-7*, 159
Lamb & Artichoke Stew 164, *165*
Gluten-free Orange & Almond
Cake *230-1, 231*
Green Lentil & Rice Salad 186, *187*
green vegetables: Braised Greens in
Olive Oil 110, *111*

## H

*Habar bil Toum wa Leymoon 148, 149*
*Habar Maklee 74, 75*
*Halloumi bil Za'atar 84, 85*
halloumi cheese *see* cheese
*Halloumi Meshwy bil Banadoura 102,*
*103*
halva: Comptoir Spiced Hot
Chocolate with Tahina &
Halva 239
harissa 13
Spiced Fried Squid with Harissa
Sauce 74, *75*
*Hindbe Belzeyt 110, 111*
Hommos: Beetroot Hommos *54-5,*
57

Classic Hommos *54-5*, 56
Hommos Beiruty *54-5*, 57
Hommos with Lamb & Pine Nuts
*54-5*, 57
Red Pepper Hommos *54-5, 57*
honey 13
Feta with Sesame Seeds & Honey
*22-3*, 25
Labneh with Caramelised
Poached Quinces & Spiced Dried
Fruit 40, *41*
My Roasted Aubergine, Rose,
Honey & Labneh Tart *233, 234-5*
Walnut & Cinnamon Honey
Cigars *228, 229*

## I

ingredients 11-15

## J

*Jawaneh 72, 73*

## K

*Kaak bil Semssoum* 50
*Kaak bil Tamar 43, 44-5*
kaak sticks 238
*Kabab Hindi 132-3, 133-4*
*Kasbat Dojoj bil Debs el Romane 76, 77*
*Kataf Ghanam Meshwy 122-3, 124-5*
*Kebab Batnjan 136-7, 137*
kebabs: Aubergine & Spiced
Minced-Lamb Kebabs *136-7,*
*137*
Monkfish & Roasted Pepper
Kebab 153
*Kelb el Louz 218, 219*
*Kharshoof bil Tahina 65, 67*
*Khobz* 51
*Kibab Samak* 153
*Kibbe Banadoura 198, 199*
*Kibbe Saynieh 190-1, 191*
*Kibet Batata bil Saynieh 178-9, 179*
*Kofta bil Saynieh 166-7, 167*
koftas: Spiced Lamb Koftas with
Potatoes & Tomatoes *166-7, 167*
*Koosa bil Tahina 61, 63*
*Koussa bil Laban 172, 173*
*Kunefe 208, 209*

## L

labneh: Date, Almond, Orange
Blossom Smoothie *240-1*, 242

Labneh & Caramelised Banana
Wrap 38, *39*
Labneh Dip 58, *59*
Labneh with Caramelised
Poached Quinces & Spiced
Dried Fruit 40, *41*
Lebanese Village Breakfast *30-1*,
32
My Roasted Aubergine, Rose,
Honey & Labneh Tart *233,*
*234-5*
*Labneh bil Safarjal Meshwy 40, 41*
lamb: Aubergine & Spiced
Minced-Lamb Kebabs *136-7,*
*137*
Baby Aubergines with Spiced
Minced Lamb & Tahina *168-9,*
*170-1*
Bulgar Wheat & Spiced Minced
Lamb Pie *190-1, 191*
Hommos with Lamb & Pine Nuts
*54-5*, 57
Lamb & Artichoke Stew 164, *165*
Potato & Spiced Minced Lamb
Pie *178-9, 179*
Scrambled Eggs with Lamb &
Courgettes 36, *37*
Slow-Cooked Shoulder of Lamb
*122-3, 124-5*
Spiced Lamb Koftas with
Potatoes & Tomatoes *166-7, 167*
Spiced Lamb Pastries 78, *79*
Spiced Meatballs in Tomato
Sauce *132-3, 133-4*
Stuffed Cabbage Leaves with
Spiced Minced Lamb & Rice
200, *201*
Stuffed Courgettes in a Yoghurt
Sauce 172, *173*
Stuffed Peppers with Spiced Rice
& Lamb 182, *183*
Lebanese Chicken Soup 162, *163*
Lebanese Lemonade 245
Lebanese seven-spice mix 13
Lebanese Village Breakfast *30-1*,
*32-3*
lemon: Baby Chicken with Lemon
Juice & Potatoes 128, *129*
Cuttlefish with Garlic, Lemon &
Coriander 148, *149*
Frozen Mint Lemonade *240-1*,
243
Lebanese Lemonade 245
Lentil Soup with Lemon *156-7,*
158

Vanilla Citronnade 244
Watermelon Lemonade *240-1*,
243
lentils 14
Green Lentil & Rice Salad 186, *187*
Lentil Soup with Lemon *156-7*,
158
liver: Chicken Livers with Cherry
Tomatoes & Pomegranate
Molasses 76, *77*
*Loubia Belzeyt* 106, *107*

## M

*Mahshi Malfouf* 200, *201*
*Mahshi Sekek* 192-3, *194-5*
*Mahshy Felfel* 182, *183*
*Makalee Khodar* 68, 69
*Maklouba* 184, *185*
*Man'ousha Banadora bil Za'atar* 46-7,
48
*Man'ousha Sabanegh wa Jabnat al Feta*
46-7, 49
mascarpone cheese: Tahina,
Chocolate & Pistachio
Cheesecake *210-11*, 212
*Mashroob Hadj Chabane 240-1*, 242
meatballs: Spiced Lamb Koftas with
Potatoes & Tomatoes 166-7, *167*
Spiced Meatballs in Tomato
Sauce *132-3*, 133-4
menus 246-9
milk: Comptoir Spiced Hot
Chocolate with Tahina &
Halva 239
Date, Almond, Orange Blossom &
Labneh Smoothie *240-1*, 242
Sahlab 238
mint 14
Fresh Mint & Orange Blossom
Tea 236
Frozen Mint Lemonade *240-1*,
243
Ful Salad with Radish & Mint
112, *113*
Tomato & Mint Soup *163*, 161
Monkfish & Roasted Pepper Kebab
153
*Moudardara* 186, *187*
*Moufaraket Koussa* 36, *37*
*Mougharabieh Dajaj* 202-3, 204-5
Mouhalabiah, Rose 214, *215*
*Moussabaha* 174, *175*
*Moussakhan* 130, *131*
*Moutabag Ashta* 220, *221*

*Muhamara Hallabyah* 70
My Big Fat Feast 247
My Mum Zohra's Fried Sardines
146-7, *147*
My Roasted Aubergine, Rose,
Honey & Labneh Tart *233*, 234-5

## N

nigella seeds 14
Feta & Nigella Seed Falafel 82, *83*
noodles: Lebanese Chicken Soup
162, *163*
nuts 14
Aleppo Roast Peppers & Mixed
Nut Dip 70
*see also* almonds, walnuts *etc*

## O

okra: Braised Okra with Tomato
Sauce 116, *117*
olive oil 14
olives: Lebanese Village Breakfast
*30-1*, 32
Pastries Stuffed with Olives 80,
*81*
Omelette, Aubergine & Halloumi
20, *21*
onions: Giant Couscous with
Chicken *202-3*, 204-5
Monkfish & Roasted Pepper
Kebab 153
Palestinian Braised Spiced
Chicken Pie 130, *131*
Roasted Chicken & Couscous
Salad 86-7, *87*
Stuffed Swiss Chard with Spiced
Rice & Vegetables *192-3*, 194-5
orange blossom water 15
Café Blanc 237
Date, Almond, Orange Blossom &
Labneh Smoothie *240-1*, 242
Fresh Mint & Orange Blossom
Tea 236
Frozen Mint Lemonade *240-1*,
243
Lebanese Lemonade 245
Semolina, Almond & Orange
Blossom Honey Cake 218, *219*
Watermelon Lemonade *240-1*,
243
oranges: Gluten-free Orange &
Almond Cake 230-1, *231*
Lebanese Lemonade 245

## P

Palestinian Braised Spiced Chicken
Pie 130, *131*
Palestinian Spiced Rice with
Chicken 184, *185*
paprika 14
parsley: Tabbouleh 144, *145*
pastries: Crisp Filo Parcels with
Cream & Rose Water 220, *221*
Pastries Stuffed with Feta &
Halloumi or Olives 80, *81*
Spiced Lamb Pastries 78, *79*
Walnut & Cinnamon Honey
Cigars 228, *229*
Zallabia 222, *223*
*see also* pies; tarts
peas: Lamb & Artichoke Stew 164,
*165*
peppercorns 11
peppers: Aleppo Roast Peppers &
Mixed Nut Dip 70
Aubergine & Spiced Minced-
Lamb Kebabs 136-7, *137*
Butter Bean Salad 96, *97*
Monkfish & Roasted Pepper
Kebab 153
Palestinian Spiced Rice with
Chicken 184, *185*
Red Pepper Hommos *54-5*, 57
Roasted Chicken & Couscous
Salad 86-7, *87*
Roasted Pepper & Feta Salad *113*,
114, *115*
Roasted Pepper Salad 94, *95*
Spiced Meatballs in Tomato
Sauce *132-3*, 133-4
Spiced Roast Chicken 126, *127*
Stuffed Peppers with Spiced Rice
& Lamb 182, *183*
pickles: Lebanese Village Breakfast
*30-1*, 32
pies: Bulgar Wheat & Spiced
Minced Lamb Pie 190-1, *191*
Palestinian Braised Spiced
Chicken Pie 130, *131*
Potato & Spiced Minced Lamb
Pie 178-9, *179*
*see also* pastries; tarts
pine nuts: Hommos with Lamb &
Pine Nuts *54-5*, 57
Potato & Spiced Minced Lamb
Pie 178-9, *179*
pistachio nuts: Feta with Pistachios
& Date Syrup *22-3*, 25

INDEX

Fig, Halloumi & Pistachio Tart 224-5, 226-7
Pomegranate & Pistachio Cheesecake 210-11, 213
Tahina, Chocolate & Pistachio Cheesecake 210-11, 212
pomegranate molasses 14
Chicken Livers with Cherry Tomatoes & Pomegranate Molasses 76, 77
pomegranate seeds: Aubergine & Pomegranate Salad 92, 93
Pomegranate & Pistachio Cheesecake 210-11, 213
potatoes: Baby Chicken with Lemon Juice & Potatoes 128, 129
New Potatoes & Green Tahina Salad 98, 99
Potato & Spiced Minced Lamb Pie 178-9, 179
Seafood Stew 142, 143
Spiced Lamb Koftas with Potatoes & Tomatoes 166-7, 167
Spiced Potatoes 71
Stuffed Swiss Chard with Spiced Rice & Vegetables 192-3, 194-5
praline: Semolina, Almond & Orange Blossom Honey Cake 218, 219
prawns: Sautéed Prawns with Spiced Braised Fennel 152
Seafood Stew 142, 143
Pumpkin & Saffron Soup 156-7, 160

Q

The Quick Feast 248
quinces: Labneh with Caramelised Poached Quinces & Spiced Dried Fruit 40, 41

R

radishes: Ful Salad with Radish & Mint 112, 113
red mullet: Fried Red Mullet with Crisp Bread & Tahina 144, 145
Red Pepper Hommos 54-5, 57
rice 15
Green Lentil & Rice Salad 186, 187
Palestinian Spiced Rice with Chicken 184, 185
Sea Bass with Spiced Rice 150, 151
Slow-Cooked Shoulder of Lamb 122-3, 124-5
Stuffed Cabbage Leaves with

Spiced Minced Lamb & Rice 200, 201
Stuffed Courgettes in a Yoghurt Sauce 172, 173
Stuffed Peppers with Spiced Rice & Lamb 182, 183
Stuffed Swiss Chard with Spiced Rice & Vegetables 192-3, 194-5
rose water 15
Crisp Filo Parcels with Cream & Rose Water 220, 221
Lebanese Lemonade 245
My Roasted Aubergine, Rose, Honey & Labneh Tart 233, 234-5
Rose Mouhalabiah with Summer Fruit Compote 214, 215
Shredded Filo & Cheese Pudding with a Rose-Honey Syrup 208, 209

S

saffron: Pumpkin & Saffron Soup 156-7, 160
Sahlab 238
salads: Aubergine & Pomegranate Salad 92, 93
Beetroot, Fig & Feta Salad 104, 105
Bulgar Wheat & Tomato Salad 198, 199
Butter Bean Salad 96, 97
Ful Salad with Radish & Mint 112, 113
Green Lentil & Rice Salad 186, 187
Grilled Chopped Aubergine Salad 90, 91
New Potatoes & Green Tahina Salad 98, 99
Roasted Chicken & Couscous Salad 86-7, 87
Roasted Pepper & Feta Salad 113, 114, 115
Roasted Pepper Salad 94, 95
Tabbouleh 144, 145
Village Tomato Salad 100, 101
Salatete Banadoura 100, 101
Salatete Batata bil Tahina Khadra 98, 99
Salatete Batenjan 118
Salatete Batenjan bil Romane 92, 93
Salatete Couscous bil Dajaj 86-7, 87
Salatete el Raheb 90, 91
Salatete Fassoulieh Beyda 96, 97
Salatete Felafela Meshwy 113, 115
Salatete Ful 112, 113

Salatete Meshwiya 94, 95
Salatete Shoumandar wa Teen 104, 105
salmon: Seafood Stew 142, 143
salt 15
Samboussek 80, 81
sardines: My Mum Zohra's Fried Sardines 146-7, 147
sausages: Sujuk Scrambled Eggs 26, 27
Sayadieh 150, 151
Saynia Dajaj wa Batata 128, 129
sea bass: Sea Bass with Spiced Rice 150, 151
Seafood Stew 142, 143
sea bream: Baked Bream with Tahina Sauce 140, 141
Seafood Stew 142, 143
Semolina, Almond & Orange Blossom Honey Cake 218, 219
sesame seeds 15
Date Brioche 43, 44-5
Feta with Sesame Seeds & Honey 22-3, 25
Sesame Seed Bread 50
seven-spice mix 13
Sfeeha 78, 79
Shakshuka Batenjan 18, 19
Shay bil Naânaâ 236
Shorbat Adas bil Hamood 156-7, 158
Shorbat Banadora wa Naânâa 156-7, 161
Shorbat Dajaj 162, 163
Shorbat Kharshoof bil Tahina 156-7, 159
Shorbat Lakteen wa Zaafrane 156-7, 160
Shredded Filo & Cheese Pudding 208, 209
soups: Artichoke & Tahina Soup 156-7, 159
Lebanese Chicken Soup 162, 163
Lentil Soup with Lemon 156-7, 158
Pumpkin & Saffron Soup 156-7, 160
Tomato & Mint Soup 163, 161
Spiced Potatoes 71
spices 11-15
spinach: Feta & Spinach Flatbreads 46-7, 49
spring onions: Feta with Tomatoes & Spring Onions 22-3, 24
squash: Pumpkin & Saffron Soup 156-7, 160
Roasted Chicken & Couscous Salad 86-7, 87
squid: Seafood Stew 142, 143

Spiced Fried Squid with Harissa
    Sauce 74, 75
stews: Chicken & Chickpea Stew
    176, 177
    Lamb & Artichoke Stew 164, 165
    Seafood Stew 142, 143
Sujuk Scrambled Eggs 26, 27
Sultan Ibrahim 144, 145
sultanas: Sweet Potato & Tahina
    Pudding 216, 217
sumac 15
Summer Feast 248
Sweet Potato & Tahina Pudding
    216, 217
Swiss chard: Braised Greens in
    Olive Oil 110, 111
    Lentil Soup with Lemon 156-7,
    158
    Stuffed Swiss Chard with Spiced
    Rice & Vegetables 192-3, 194-5
Syrian Aubergine Salad 118

**T**

Tabbouleh 144, 145
tahina 15
    Artichoke & Tahina Soup 156-7,
    159
    Artichoke Heart & Tahina Dip
    65, 67
    Aubergine & Walnut Dip 61, 62
    Baby Aubergines with Spiced
    Minced Lamb & Tahina 168-9,
    170-1
    Baked Bream with Tahina Sauce
    140, 141
    Broad Bean & Tahina Dip
    65, 66
    Cauliflower & Tahina 119
    Chickpeas with Yoghurt &
    Tahina Sauce 174, 175
    Classic Hommos 54-5, 56
    Comptoir Spiced Hot Chocolate
    with Tahina & Halva 239
    Courgette & Tahina Dip 61, 63
    New Potatoes & Green Tahina
    Salad 98, 99
    Sweet Potato & Tahina Pudding
    216, 217
    Tahina, Chocolate & Pistachio
    Cheesecake 210-11, 212
    Tahina Sauce 144, 145
    Yoghurt & Tahina Sauce 68, 69
Tajen Samak 140, 141
Tarator Sauce 119
Tartine, Fig & Feta 28, 29

tarts: Fig, Halloumi & Pistachio Tart
    224-5, 226-7
    My Roasted Aubergine, Rose,
    Honey & Labneh Tart 233, 234-5
Tea, Fresh Mint & Orange Blossom
    236
tomatoes: Aubergine Shakshuka
    18, 19
    Beetroot, Fig & Feta Salad 104, 105
    Braised Okra with Tomato Sauce
    116, 117
    Broad Beans in a Tomato Sauce
    34, 35
    Bulgar Wheat & Tomato Salad
    198, 199
    Chicken Livers with Cherry
    Tomatoes & Pomegranate
    Molasses 76, 77
    Feta with Tomatoes & Spring
    Onions 22-3, 24
    French Beans in a Tomato &
    Olive Oil Sauce 106, 107
    Grilled Halloumi with Roasted
    Vine Tomatoes 102, 103
    Labneh Dip 58, 59
    Monkfish & Roasted Pepper
    Kebab 153
    Sautéed Prawns with Spiced
    Braised Fennel 152
    Seafood Stew 142, 143
    Slow-Cooked Shoulder of Lamb
    122-3, 124-5
    Spiced Lamb Koftas with
    Potatoes & Tomatoes 166-7, 167
    Spiced Lamb Pastries 78, 79
    Spiced Meatballs in Tomato
    Sauce 132-3, 133-4
    Spiced Tomato Flatbreads 46-7,
    48
    Stuffed Swiss Chard with Spiced
    Rice & Vegetables 192-3, 194-5
    Sujuk Scrambled Eggs 26, 27
    Syrian Aubergine Salad 118
    Tabbouleh 144, 145
    Tomato & Mint Soup 163, 161
    Village Tomato Salad 100, 101

**V**

Vanilla Citronnade 244
vegetables: Fried Vegetables with
    Yoghurt & Tahina Sauce 68, 69
    Lebanese Village Breakfast 30-1,
    33
    see also aubergines, peppers etc
Vegetarian Feast 249

vermicelli pasta: Lebanese Chicken
    Soup 162, 163
Village Tomato Salad 100, 101
vinegar, cider 12

**W**

walnuts: Aubergine & Walnut Dip
    61, 62
    Walnut & Cinnamon Honey
    Cigars 228, 229
Watermelon Lemonade 240-1, 243
Weekend feast 246-7
Wrap, Labneh & Caramelised
    Banana 38, 39

**Y**

Yaknatt Dajaj bil Hommos 176, 177
Yaknatt el Kharshoof bil Laham 164, 165
Yaknatt Semar al Bahar 142, 143
yoghurt: Aubergine & Walnut Dip
    61, 62
    Baby Aubergines with Spiced
    Minced Lamb & Tahina 168-9,
    170-1
    Chickpeas with Yoghurt &
    Tahina Sauce 174, 175
    Courgette & Tahina Dip 61, 63
    Cucumber & Yoghurt Sauce 191
    Freekeh with Chicken 196, 197
    My Roasted Aubergine, Rose,
    Honey & Labneh Tart 233, 234-5
    Stuffed Courgettes in a Yoghurt
    Sauce 172, 173
    Yoghurt & Tahina Sauce 68, 69

**Z**

za'atar 15
    Feta with Olive Oil & Za'atar
    22-3, 25
    Za'atar-crusted Halloumi 84, 85
Zallabia 222, 223

## ACKNOWLEDGEMENTS

I'd like to thank Chaker Hanna – my friend, brother, father, confidant and business partner. We laughed and cried together and now work hard together. He gives me the freedom to keep being creative and doing what I really love.

My assistant, Kasia, who knows me better than anyone. Huge thanks for keeping my life running smoothly, you're wonderful!

To all the teams in all our restaurants, past and present – I owe it all to you, whom I consider my family. It is the labour of love of every team member that made all this all possible.

Wassim Al Sammour, for his passion, ideas and contributions to the book. He continues to help me discover new Syrian dishes and cooks some of the best Arabic food I've ever eaten. Thanks to Mohamed Ourad, for your support. Talal Al Endari, for enormous help generating new ideas. Firas Marouf, you get into my head and make my sweet dreams reality.

Jerome Guermah, for supporting us whatever we need. Jad Youssef, for helping with the incredible Lebanese recipes. Soufiane Bennis, for allowing me into Levant's kitchen when working on our book. Conrad Patterson, for your passion and love for our family, food and hospitality. I'm grateful to Lesley McIlroy and Tim Warner, too.

My brothers and sister for giving me all the hassle and love siblings should. Thank you for making me want to lead by example. I must mention my brother Mehdi, for working with us tirelessly for 17 years; my sister-in-law Lynda, for your patience even when I drive you crazy and for looking after my decorations storeroom. My brother Salah, who is still recovering from his head injury, and his long-term partner Rita, the most caring woman I've met.

Thanks to Nicola Ibison, my friend and agent, for believing in me from the start; for your guidance and telling me off when I needed it.

At HarperCollins: Rachel Kenny and Lisa Milton, who've been so patient – you helped me make a book I'm very proud of, and Sarah Hammond, for being the most organized person I've ever met.

Emma Marsden, for being so patient testing all the recipes, Mary-Jane Wilkins for skilful copyediting, and Kat Mead, for helping me express my crazy journey.

To Louise McGrory, Anita Mangan, Phillipa Langley, Olivia Wardle, Rosie Ramsden and Liam Baker for bringing these recipes and everything contained within them to life with such warmth.

My friends: Tooba, for her support and putting up with me. Haleem, who drives me mad and always gets me in trouble. Jonathan, Adam and Sam Kaye, for holding our hands when it mattered. Richard Kleiner, for being an amazing advisor.

Mamdouh, Amr and the Moteia Ismail family, for always being there – you've been amazing support. Haj Abdelhaq, who has helped source the best from the Marrakech souks for 19 years. Daphne and Avi Lerner, for giving me aspiration in life. Dan Lepard and David Whitehouse, for the encouragement. Ziad El Akabi, for your help; Marhoune Rougab, for running races in the desert with me. Yonatan Yigzaw, for helping me stay fit and healthy. Thanks to all my other friends who are too shy to be mentioned.

It is with enormous gratitude I thank our guests, whose love of Middle Eastern flavours grows stronger every day and without whom our family has no one to feed.

No thank you is complete without mentioning my mother, Zohra, my rock, soul and drive. She's been with me at every step. And my father, Haj Chabane, who is no longer with us. I still miss him and wish he were here to see the results of the hard work. They gave me their blessing and the permission to dream and they supported me through it all. Thank you for continuing to inspire me every day.